W9-CBI-686

Batsford Chess Library

The Young Pretenders

Who will be the next World Chess Champion?

International Grandmaster
Raymond Keene

An Owl Book
Henry Holt and Company
New York

THE YOUNG PRETENDERS

Henry Holt and Company, Inc.
Publishers since 1866
115 West 18th Street
New York, New York 10011

Henry Holt® is a registered trademark
of Henry Holt and Company, Inc.

Copyright © 1994 by Raymond Keene
All rights reserved.
First published in the United States in 1994 by
Henry Holt and Company, Inc.
Originally published in Great Britain in 1994 by
B. T. Batsford Ltd.

Library of Congress Catalog Card Number: 94-77370

ISBN 0-8050-3291-6 (An Owl Book: pbk.)

First American Edition—1994

Printed in the United Kingdom
All first editions are printed on acid-free paper. ∞

10 9 8 7 6 5 4 3 2 1

Adviser: R. D. Keene, GM, OBE
Technical Editor: Graham Burgess

Contents

Algebraic Notation

The moves contained in this book are given in what is known as 'Figurine Algebraic' notation. This somewhat complicated-sounding term actually describes a very simple way of writing down the moves. Readers familiar with the system can jump ahead to the games themselves, but those who are comparatively new to the game or who have only learned the older 'English Descriptive' notation will find what follows helpful. It is assumed that the reader already knows how to *play* chess.

Each piece is represented by a symbol, called a 'Figurine', as follows:

Pawn	♙
Knight	♘
Bishop	♗
Rook	♖
Queen	♕
King	♔

The squares on the chessboard are described by coordinates, consisting of a letter followed by a number (see diagram). For instance the square marked with a cross is called 'e4'. This follows exactly the same principle as reading off a reference on an A-Z street guide or road map.

Chess Symbols
The following are the most frequently used chess symbols: + - check; ! - good move; !! - brilliant move; ? - bad move; ?? - blunder; !? - interesting move; ?! - dubious move; ol - Olympiad; izt - Interzonal; zt - Zonal.

Introduction

The Year of the Three Emperors

The year 69AD was both a confusing and an exciting one for the Roman Empire. No less than four claimants, Galba, Otho, Vitellius and Vespasian, declared themselves Emperor. The year 1993 was similarly exciting and confusing for the world of chess. According to the newly-established Professional Chess Association (PCA), Garry Kasparov was world champion. If you were to believe FIDE (the World Chess Federation) then Anatoly Karpov would be the champion. Indeed, Karpov's superb result at the Linares tournament early in 1994, ahead of most of the players in this book, confirmed his aspirations in the eyes of many. Finally, the enigmatic and mercurial Bobby Fischer, never defeated since he had wrested the title from Boris Spassky in 1972, had returned to chess and had announced that he too considered himself world champion.

This book details the career, analyses the style and assesses the prospects of each of the players who might challenge for the world title in years to come or, indeed, unify the various titles which are at stake. To my mind, though, no-one can be legitimately considered world champion, unless Garry Kasparov is first defeated in a set match. He who would be Emperor must cross the Rubicon and go directly to Rome.

Who has the best chance of achieving this? Ivanchuk and Shirov, both great players, suffer excessively from nerves. They will find it difficult to propel themselves through qualifying competitions. Nigel Short now has more experience than most, but suffers from the disparity of performing brilliantly with White but less impressively with Black. Fischer will probably never play Kasparov, while Karpov, if he insists on adhering solely to the closed orbit of FIDE competitions, may inflict the same fate on himself. Never in the history of world championship play has a female grandmaster challenged for the highest honours. Nevertheless, this possibility can no longer be ruled out. In speed play,

Judit Polgar, the Hungarian girl prodigy, has proved herself the equal of the greatest, while at the Madrid tournament of May 1994 she substantially outperformed four of the world's top ten rated players, including Shirov and Kamsky. The odds must be against it, but her chances cannot be ignored.

Such equations leave only the brilliantly talented Vladimir Kramnik and the iron-nerved Indian, Viswanathan Anand. Since both are competing in the PCA as well as FIDE cycles, the chance must exist that one of these two very different players may succeed in emerging from both parallel championships to challenge Kasparov. This could unify the PCA and FIDE versions of the world championship title.

The PCA and FIDE not only run separate and parallel world championships, but also publish their own distinct rating lists. It may assist in predicting the future prospects of those covered in this book, to compare the top ten of both lists. It should be noted that FIDE, after the PCA split away from them, refuse to publish ratings either for Kasparov or for Short.

	PCA list		FIDE list	
1	Kasparov	2808	Karpov	2781
2	Karpov	2797	Shirov	2727
3	Shirov	2716	Anand	2721
4	Anand	2714	Kramnik	2716
5	Ivanchuk	2708	Salov	2711
6	Salov	2708	Ivanchuk	2704
7	Kramnik	2697	Bareev	2699
8	Bareev	2687	Kamsky	2695
9	Short	2686	Gelfand	2685
10	Gelfand	2676	Epishin	2675

1 Garry Kasparov - The Czar of the Chess Empire

Player's Name: Garry Kasparov
Date of Birth: 13 April 1963
Nationality: Russian
Main Strengths
Superb memory and grasp of theory, supremely persistent and determined, a demon of hard work and preparation, with a unique feel for the initiative and attack.
Main Weaknesses
Occasional relaxation due to over-confidence. Sometimes distracted by his political ambitions in Russia.

Kasparov dominated the 1992 Linares tournament. This annual competition is regarded as the Wimbledon of chess.

Linares 1992
Kasparov 10/13; Ivanchuk, Timman 8; Karpov 7½; Anand, Salov, Gelfand 7; Bareev 6½; Beliavsky, Yusupov 6; Illescas 5½; Ljubojevic 4½; Speelman, Short 4.

Here is Kasparov's victory against his arch-rival.

Kasparov - Karpov
Caro-Kann Defence
Linares 1992

1	e4	c6
2	d4	d5
3	♘d2	dxe4
4	♘xe4	♘d7
5	♘g5	♘gf6
6	♗c4	e6
7	♕e2	♘b6
8	♗b3	h6
9	♘5f3 (1)	

| 9 | ... | c5 |

Two years later, Karpov tried to improve his play here: 9 ... a5 10 c3 c5 11 a3 ♕c7 12 ♘e5 cxd4

13 cxd4 was Kasparov – Karpov, Linares 1994, and now Karpov missed 13 ... ♗xa3! which would have snatched a vital pawn, e.g. 14 ♖xa3 ♕xc1+ or 14 bxa3 ♕xc3+. A most surprising twist, overlooked by both players!

10	♗f4	♗d6

This is passive and should be replaced by 10 ... ♘bd5 11 ♗e5 ♕a5+ 12 ♘d2 b5 with vigorous counterplay as in three games by Speelman against Sax, Nunn and Short from 1988.

11	♗g3	♕e7
12	dxc5	♗xc5
13	♘e5	♗d7
14	♘gf3	♘h5
15	0-0-0	♘xg3
16	hxg3	0-0-0

Black's king is not entirely safe on the queenside where he is missing the shelter of the c-pawn, but with an open h-file it would clearly be too dangerous to castle on the other wing.

17	♖h5 *(2)*	

An original way to activate his rook which is actually straining to reach the queen-side.

17	...	♕e8
18	♖xd8+	♔xd8
19	♕d2+	♗d6
20	♘d3	♕c7
21	g4	♔c8
22	g5	♗f8
23	♖h4	♔b8
24	a4 *(3)*	

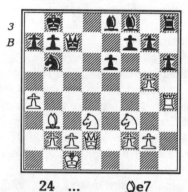

24	...	♗e7

According to Kasparov this is the decisive mistake. Black must hinder the further advance of White's a-pawn, hence 24 ... a6 was the correct move.

25	a5	♘d5
26	♔b1	

White is now threatening 27 c4 which would trap Black's knight in the middle of the board.

26	...	♘d8

I have observed that in recent games against Kasparov, Karpov has adopted a somewhat Steinitzian policy of defence in depth by retreating his pieces into seemingly impregnable defensive dug-outs. Here, his king is exposed and his pieces have been driven spectacularly back. Karpov was, though, probably hoping that his bishop pair would eventually emerge to rule the earth.

27 a6

Well aware that Black still has long term advantages in his favour, Kasparov is swift to drive home his assault.

27	...	♛a5
28	♕e2	♞b6

28 ... ♕xa6 is impossible on account of 29 ♕e5+ ♚a8 30 ♕xg7.

29 axb7 *(4)*

With Karpov having failed to prevent the advance of this pawn it now rips away the last vestiges of defence around the black king.

29	...	♗xg5
30	♞xg5	♕xg5
31	♖h5	♕f6
32	♖a5	♗c6
33	♞c5	

Threatening ♖xa7 followed by ♕a6+. Black must, therefore, permit the exchange of one of the pieces which is still defending his king.

| 33 | ... | ♗xb7 |

34	♞xb7	♚xb7
35	♕a6+	♚c6
36	♗a4+	♚d6
37	♕d3+	*(5)*

Black's case is hopeless. White could win a piece in a number of ways hereabouts, but prefers to play for mate.

37	...	♞d5
38	♕g3+	

Kasparov does not even bother to win a piece with 38 c4.

38	...	♕e5
39	♕a3+	♚c7
40	♕c5+	♚d8
41	♖xa7	*(6)*

Black resigned

His king is hopelessly exposed.

Russia scored an over-whelming victory in the 1992 Manila Olympics some months after Linares. The magnitude of their success can be gauged from the fact that Kasparov's team had secured the gold medals with one round to spare. Kasparov himself was a superb inspiration to the re-mainder of his team, scoring an unbeaten 85% from his first ten games. With a powerhouse like that at the front, it is under-standable that the rest of the squad was spurred on to a superlative effort.

Kasparov did not just score well, he also produced a num-ber of gems of chess strategy, during the course of which he despatched such promising young rivals as Kamsky (USA), Shirov (Latvia) and Ivanchuk (Ukraine). The win against Ivanchuk was one of Kasparov's most subtle achievements:

Kasparov - Ivanchuk
Manila Olympiad 1992
English Opening

1 ♘f3

One of the hallmarks of Kasparov's opening repertoire is its great flexibility. When the young Kasparov was ascending the ladder to the world cham-pionship he was almost ex-clusively a 1 d4 player. Now, however, he has broadened his arsenal to include 1 e4 and the manifold subtleties of the various flank openings, of which this is one.

1	...	c5
2	c4	♘c6
3	♘c3	♘f6
4	g3	d6
5	♗g2	g6
6	d4	cxd4
7	♘xd4	(7)

This particular variation reached prominence in the celebrated 8th game of the Fischer - Spassky match at Reykjavik 1972. At that time, though, the continuation was 7 ... ♘xd4 8 ♛xd4 ♗g7 9 0-0 0-0 10 ♗g5, with an eventual White win.

7	...	♗d7
8	e4	♗g7
9	♘xc6	♗xc6

The Ukranian Grandmaster would doubtless have preferred strengthen his pawn centre by playing 9 ... bxc6. In that eventuality, though, he would have had to take into account the dangerous pawn sacrifice 10 c5!. After 10 ... dxc5 Black's pawn centre has been demolished and White would easily regain the weak pawn on c5.

10	♗e3	0-0
11	0-0	a5
12	♖c1	a4
13	♕e2	♕a5
14	♖fd1	♖fc8
15	c5!	*(8)*

Exactly the same motif as adumbrated in my previous comment. If Black plays 15 ... dxc5 then 16 e5 ♘e8 17 ♗xc6 ♖xc6 18 ♘d5 leaves Black in some difficulties for which his extra pawn is inadequate recompense.

15	...	♘e8
16	cxd6	♘xd6
17	♘d5	

White's threats have now become so intense that Ivanchuk is forced to cede his great opponent the advantage of the bishop pair.

17	...	♗xd5
18	♖xd5	♖xc1+
19	♗xc1	♕c7
20	♗f4	♕c4
21	♕xc4	♘xc4 *(9)*

The exchange of queens appears to have alleviated

Black's problems to the extent that he can reasonably hope for a draw. However, there now ensues an amusing hunt of Black's knight by White's b-pawn which concludes with White still enjoying a slight advantage.

22	b3	axb3
23	axb3	♘a5

If instead 23 ... ♖a1+ 24 ♔f1 ♘a5 25 ♖d8+ ♔f8 26 ♗h6 and Black faces checkmate.

24	b4	♘c6
25	b5	♘d4
26	♗f1	h5
27	♔g2	♘c2 *(10)*

Ivanchuk offers stout resistance, but on an open board the bishops dominate Black's knight and Black still has to worry about the weakness of his own b-pawn.

28	♗d2	e6
29	♖c5	♘d4
30	♗e3	b6
31	♖c7	♖a1
32	♖c8+	

With the time control at move 40 Kasparov clearly wanted to gain some time on the clock. Otherwise, he could have played ♖c4 at once as he does two moves later.

32	...	♔h7
33	♖c7	♔g8
34	♖c4	*(11)*

11
B

Black's knight is embarrassed for squares for if 34 ... ♘xb5 35 ♖c8+ and ♗xb5 winning a piece.

| 34 | ... | ♖d1 |

This way of defending his knight also has its disadvantages, but if instead 34 ... e5 then 35 ♖c8+ ♔h7 36 ♗c4 when Black's position falls apart.

| 35 | ♖c8+ | ♔h7 |
| 36 | ♖d8 | |

Now Black is in a deadly pin. Essentially Black's rook, knight

and bishop are all immobilized and it only remains for White to play ♗e2 at some opportune moment and the whole rickety structure will come tumbling down.

36	...	♗e5
37	h3	♔g7
38	♗c4	♔f6
39	♖d7	g5

Apart from this Black is devoid of constructive moves.

| 40 | ♗e2 | |

If now 40 ... ♖e1 then 41 ♗xh5 wins easily enough. Therefore Black is forced to give up material.

40	...	♘xe2
41	♖xd1	♘c3
42	♖d8	♘xe4
43	♗xb6	♘c3
44	♖g8	♘xb5
45	♗d8+	

Black resigned, since 45 ... ♔f5 46 ♖xg5+ is utterly hopeless for him.

Kamsky – Kasparov
Manila Olympiad 1992
King's Indian Defence

1	d4	♘f6
2	c4	g6
3	♘c3	♗g7
4	e4	d6
5	f3	

The Sämisch Variation, switching from the the Classical, which he had used with success against Kasparov in Dortmund 1992. Doubtless Kamsky varied since he feared an improvement on Black's part.

5	...	0-0
6	♗e3	e5
7	d5	c6
8	♕d2	cxd5
9	cxd5	a6
10	♗d3	♘h5
11	g4	(12)

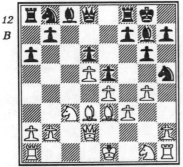

So far standard play but this is an extraordinary gesture which every Russian schoolboy knows to be bad. White drives the black knight to f4, which is precisely where it wants to go. White can normally pick up a pawn after this, but Black gains such enormous control of the dark squares in compensation and unleashes such fiery energy from his fianchettoed king's bishop that the transaction is scarcely worth it. Was this hypnotism or does Kamsky really just make up his openings as he goes along?

11	...	♘f4
12	♗c2	b5
13	♕f2	♘d7
14	♘ge2	b4
15	♘a4	a5 (13)

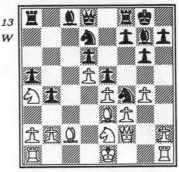

Of course Black does not bother about the pawn.

16	♘xf4	exf4
17	♗xf4	♘e5
18	0-0-0	

White's king is quite unsafe wherever it seeks refuge.

18	...	♘c4
19	♗e3	♘xe3

It is important to remove White's dark squared bishop before it can challenge the long diagonal with ♗d4.

20	♕xe3	♖b8
21	♗b3	♗d7
22	♔b1	♕e8
23	♘b6	♗b5
24	♖d2	a4
25	♗d1	♖b7
26	e5	(14)

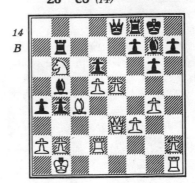

Trying to gain some breathing space by offering back the pawn. If Black accepts, which he does not, White would either gain a passed d–pawn or be able to trade queens and thus reduce the pressure.

26	...	b3
27	axb3	axb3
28	♗xb3	♕b8
29	♘c4	♗xc4
30	♗xc4	♗xe5
31	♕e2	♕a7 *(15)*

A well known strategical type of position has arisen. This is characterized by the players castling on opposite wings and opposite coloured bishops being present. Such situations normally resolve into a very easy win for the player with the attack, since he virtually has an extra piece to throw into the battle. In this case it is obvious that Black has the attack.

| 32 | ♖c1 | ♖a8 |
| 33 | b3 | ♗f4 |

This wins the exchange but Kasparov is out for more.

| 34 | ♔c2 | ♖e7 |
| 35 | ♕d3 | ♕c5 |

36	♖b1	♖e3
37	♕d4	♖a2+
38	♔d1	♖xf3 *(16)*

A very fine move. If now 39 ♕xc5 ♖xd2+ or 39 ♖xa2 ♕xd4+ and in both cases Black wins easily.

39 ♕xf4

Jettisoning White's queen does not help.

39	...	♖xf4
40	♖xa2	♕g1+
41	♔c2	♕xh2+

White resigns

The next game shows Kasparov in deadly action against one young Russian, widely tipped as a future champion himself. Previously, Kramnik had carried all before him, but when he touched his perihelion, the glare of the champion's genius disintegrated his position.

Kasparov – Kramnik
Paris Immopar 1992
Sicilian Defence

| 1 | e4 | c5 |

2 ♘f3 ♞c6
3 ♗b5

This slight deviation from the normal 3 d4 is becoming increasingly popular after the 1992 rematch between Bobby Fischer and Boris Spassky. One example from that match was game 11 which continued 3 ... g6 4 ♗xc6 bxc6 5 0–0 ♝g7 6 ♖e1 e5 and now Fischer introduced the surprisingly powerful pawn sacrifice 7 b4 and went on to secure a crushing victory. Later investigation revealed that Black could play 6 ... f6 with a fully playable position (see section on Fischer).

3 ... e6

This procedure seems somewhat less effective than a defence based on ... g6 and ... f6, as adumbrated in the previous note.

4 0–0 ♞ge7
5 c3 d5
6 exd5 ♛xd5
7 ♖e1 g6

At this point the fianchetto of Black's king's bishop is too much of a time-consuming luxury. The simple 7 ... a6 would have been preferable.

8 b4! *(17)*

A vigorous pawn sacrifice, similar in nature to the one introduced by Fischer against Spassky (see the section on Fischer). Kasparov's idea is to exploit Black's lack of development after 8 ... cxb4 9 c4 ♛d8 10 ♗b2 ♜g8 11 d4 when, at the cost of a mere pawn, White would have succeeded in thoroughly disorganizing the black camp. Kramnik prefers to decline the gambit, but still lands in hot water.

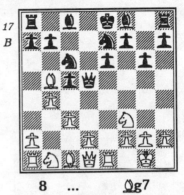

8 ... ♝g7
9 ♗b2

Setting a further cunning trap for if Black plays the seemingly innocent capture 9 ... cxb4 then 10 c4, unmasking the full power of White's bishop on b2, would lead to a decisive gain of material.

9 ... 0–0
10 c4 ♛h5
11 ♗xg7 ♚xg7
12 bxc5 ♛xc5
13 d4 *(18)*

Kasparov's opening strategy has triumphed. Not only does he dominate the centre but he has also succeeded in eliminating Black's valuable defensive dark-squared bishop. Consequently, Black's king will soon be drawn into the firing line.

13	...	♛b6
14	♞c3	♜d8
15	♗xc6	♛xc6
16	♛e2	a6
17	♜ac1	♛c7
18	d5 *(19)*	

The commencement of the final attack. Black's reply is somewhat desperate but he is faced with horrible threats such as ♞e4 followed by ♛b2+.

18	...	f6
19	dxe6	♜d6
20	♞d5	♛d8
21	♞xf6	

Completing the demolition. 21 ... ♚xf6 is of course ruled out on account of 22 ♛e5 checkmate.

21	...	♜xe6
22	♞e4	♞c6
23	♛b2+	♚g8
24	♞fg5	♜e5

| 25 | f4 | ♜f5 |
| 26 | ♜cd1 | |

Black resigned and not a moment too soon for if 26 ... ♛c7 27 ♞f6+ or 26 ... ♛e7 27 ♞d6.

Anand – Kasparov
Paris Immopar, Final,
Game 4, 1992
Sicilian Defence

1	e4	c5
2	♞f3	d6
3	d4	cxd4
4	♞xd4	♞f6
5	♞c3	a6
6	f4	♛c7

In game 2 of the final Kasparov had tried 6 ... e6 7 ♛f3 ♛b6 but lost. This is his attempt at an improvement.

7	a4	g6
8	♗d3	♗g7
9	♞f3	♞c6
10	0-0	♗g4
11	♛e1	0-0
12	♛h4	♗xf3
13	♜xf3	e6 *(20)*

This move, combined with Black's queen retreat on move

14, is an original and fascinating idea. It is based on the perception that if Black achieves the thrust ... d5 he will have an excellent position.

14	♗e3	♛d8
15	♖af1	d5
16	f5	

If White does not try this, his attack is still-born, but it appears, nevertheless, to be unsound.

16	...	dxe4
17	♖h3	exf5
18	♗xe4	

Hoping for 18 ... fxe4 19 ♖xf6, but Kasparov is not fooled by this obvious trick.

18	...	♖e8
19	♗xf5	gxf5
20	♖xf5 *(21)*	

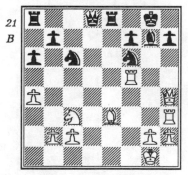

White's attack reaches its climax, but Kasparov is ready with a devastating counter.

20	...	♖xe3
21	♖xe3	♛b6
22	♛f2	

Any other move would allow ... ♖e8 intensifying the pin. The text sets a diabolical trap, but Kasparov is only too ready to

fall into it.

22	...	♘g4 *(22)*

23 ♖e8+

The point of White's trap. This wins Black's queen.

23	...	♖xe8
24	♛xb6	♗d4+

The counter-point. Kasparov wins back the queen and maintains an extra piece.

25	♛xd4	♖e1+
26	♖f1	♖xf1+
27	♔xf1	♘xd4
28	♘e4	♘xc2
29	♘c5	b5
30	a5	♘b4
31	h3	♘e3+
32	♔e2	♘c4
33	b3	♘xa5
	White resigns	

As noted before, Linares, in Spain, is the Wimbledon of chess. In 1993 Kasparov repeated his triumph of the previous year, way ahead of most of his potential rivals.

Linares 1993
Kasparov 10/13; Karpov, Anand 8½; Shirov 8; Kramnik

7½; Salov, Ivanchuk 6½; Beliavsky 6; Kamsky, Bareev 5½; Yusupov, Timman 5; Gelfand 4½; Ljubojevic 4.

Kasparov – Kamsky
Linares 1993

Kasparov faced Kamsky after he had already clinched first prize. This did not, however, deter the champion from striving for the full point.

Kasparov's next move places Black in a pin along the fourth rank - a very unusual occurrence at such an early stage of the game.

18	♖g4	h5
19	♖h4	♗c5
20	0-0-0	♗xf2
21	♘xe4	dxe4
22	♕xf2	♖c8
23	♔b1	♖d8 (24)

Due to the earlier advance of his h-pawn, Kamsky is now unable to bring his king to safety by castling. With White's queen and rook on the rampage, the extra handicap of playing with an exposed king

proves too much for Black.

24	♖xd8+	♔xd8
25	♖h3	♕d5
26	♖c3	♔d7
27	♕b6	♖d8
28	♖c5	♕d1+
29	♔a2	♔e8
30	♕xb7	♕g4
31	e6	fxe6
32	♖e5	♕g5
33	h4	♕xh4
34	♖xe6+	♔f8
35	f6 (25)	

Black resigns

The point of White's 33rd move is now apparent. If the black queen were on g5, he could exchange queens with 35 ... ♕d5+. Denied this resource, however, he has no defence against the numerous threats.

The best game from the 1993 World Championship, in which Kasparov overwhelmingly defended his title against the first ever British challenger was, ironically, a draw. One, though, which did great credit to both players:

Short – Kasparov
Times World Championship,
Game 8, London 1993
Sicilian Defence

1	e4	c5
2	♘f3	d6
3	d4	cxd4
4	♘xd4	♘f6
5	♘c3	a6
6	♗c4	e6
7	♗b3	♘bd7
8	f4	♘c5
9	e5 *(26)*	

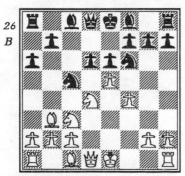

Short tries to improve on game six where he played 9 f5.

9	...	dxe5
10	fxe5	♘fd7
11	♗f4	b5
12	♕g4	h5

13	♕g3	h4
14	♕g4	g5

A risky move. Kasparov shreds his kingside pawns with the intention of wiping out White's centre.

15	0-0-0	♕e7
16	♘c6	♘xb3+
17	axb3	♕c5
18	♘e4	♕xc6
19	♗xg5	♗b7
20	♖d6 *(27)*	

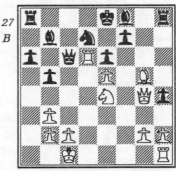

Kasparov: "A great move by Short to keep the initiative. He is a piece down so he must do something quickly."

Short: "Kasparov had overlooked this blow. If now 20 ... ♕xe4 21 ♖xe6+ fxe6 22 ♕xe6+ ♗e7 23 ♕xe7 checkmate."

20	...	♗xd6
21	♘xd6+	♔f8
22	♖f1	♘xe5
23	♕xe6	♕d5
24	♖xf7+	♘xf7
25	♗e7+	♔g7
26	♕f6+	♔h7
27	♘xf7	♕h5
28	♘g5+	♔g8
29	♕e6+	♔g7
30	♕f6+	♔g8

| 31 | ♕e6+ | ♚g7 |
| 32 | ♗f6+ | ♚h6 *(28)* |

33 ♘f7+

Kasparov: "If 33 ♕e7 then 33 ... ♖ag8 34 ♘f7+ ♚g6 35 ♘xh8+ ♖xh8 36 ♗xh8 ♕g5+ and Short's greatest possibility is to reach an ending with two pawns more, but amazingly, I can defend it, e.g. 37 ♕xg5+ ♚xg5 38 g3 hxg3 39 hxg3 ♚g4 40 ♗e5 ♗d5 41 ♚d2 ♚f3 42 ♚c3 ♗e4 and White cannot organise a passed pawn and if White doesn't play 42 ♚c3 then Black just oscillates his bishop between e6 and f7."

33	...	♚h7
34	♘g5+	♚h6
35	♗xh8+	♕g6
36	♘f7+	♚h7

| 37 | ♕e7 | ♕xg2 *(29)* |

38 ♗e5

Kasparov: "Short was in severe clock trouble here so it is not surprising that he plays a move that keeps his bishop protected. Here, however, he may have missed his one chance to win. After 38 ♗d4, the f2-square is covered and I cannot get a draw by perpetual check against Short's king, e.g. 38 ... ♕h1+ 39 ♚d2 ♕xh2+ 40 ♚c3 ♖c8+ 41 ♚b4 ♖c7 42 ♕f6 and White wins."

38	...	♕f1+
39	♚d2	♕f2+
40	♚d3	♕f3+
41	♚d2	♕f2+
	Draw	

World Championship, London 1993

	1	2	3	4	5	6	7	8	9	10	
Kasparov	1	½	1	1	½	½	1	½	1	½	
Short	0	½	0	0	½	½	0	½	0	½	

	11	12	13	14	15	16	17	18	19	20	
Kasparov	½	½	½	½	1	0	½	½	½	½	12½
Short	½	½	½	½	0	1	½	½	½	½	7½

Kasparov – Ivanchuk
Linares 1994
Semi-Slav, Anti-Meran

1	d4	♘f6
2	c4	c6
3	♘c3	d5
4	♘f3	e6
5	♗g5	dxc4
6	e4	b5
7	e5	h6
8	♗h4	g5
9	♘xg5	hxg5
10	♗xg5	♘bd7 *(30)*

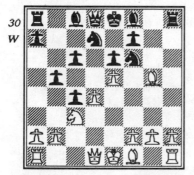

In the early 1980s Kasparov made a living out of this position but in recent years no-one has dared challenge him to a theoretical duel in this line.

11	exf6	♗b7
12	g3	c5
13	d5	♘xf6

For 13 ... ♗h6 see Kamsky – Shirov in the Shirov section. Ivanchuk tries a different path, and introduces a new idea on his next move.

14	♗g2	♗h6
15	♗xf6	♕xf6
16	0-0	0-0-0
17	♘xb5	exd5

18	♘xa7+	♔b8
19	♘b5	♗g7
20	a4	♕h6

Although Black is a pawn down, he has powerful counterplay in the h-file, as well as the bishop pair and an imposing mass of central pawns. The secret to Kasparov's victory is his ability to draw the black king itself into the firing line.

21	h4	♗f6
22	♕e1! *(31)*	

A brilliant move, ignoring Black's threat of a sacrifice on h4, in order to transfer the white queen to a5.

22	...	♗xh4
23	♕a5	♗e7

Again threatening mate on h2.

24	♕c7+	♔a8
25	♕a5+	♔b8
26	♕c7+	♔a8
27	♖fe1	

Disdaining the draw by perpetual check, whilst creating a haven for his king on f1.

27	...	♗d6
28	♕b6	♗b8
29	a5	♖d7

Of course Black cannot exchange queens with 29 ... ♛xb6 since the reply 30 axb6+ will prove ruinous for him.

30 ♖e8! *(32)*

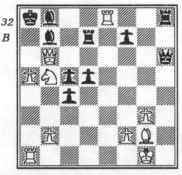

A superb irruption. Black is still denied the possibility of ... ♛xb6 while 30 ... ♖xe8 naturally fails to 31 ♛xh6. It is possible that Ivanchuk may have foreseen this brilliant coup and prepared the following queen sacrifice in advance. In spite of the ingenuity of Ivanchuk's defence it is still insufficient.

30 ... ♛h2+
31 ♔f1 ♛xg2+

31 ... ♖xe8? loses to 32 a6! ♗c8 33 ♛c6+!.

32 ♔xg2 d4+
33 ♛xb7+ *(33)*

This counter-sacrifice of the white queen breaks the back of Black's defence.

33 ... ♖xb7
34 ♖xh8 ♖xb5
35 a6 ♔a7
36 ♖f8 ♖xb2
37 ♖xf7+ ♔a8
38 a7 c3
39 ♖f8

Kasparov has conducted the technical phase with the utmost accuracy. There is now no way for Black to avoid the deadly coronation of White's a-pawn. **Black therefore resigned.**

2   Anatoly Karpov - The Old Pretender

Player's Name: Anatoly Karpov
Date of Birth: 23 May 1951
Nationality: Russian
Main Strengths
Great strategist, ability to exploit minute advantages, python-like strangulation a speciality.
Main Weaknesses
Lack of courage in extreme crisis; a tendency to sidestep modern opening theory in sharp lines.

Karpov won the World Championship without play, when Fischer defaulted in 1975. He defended it until 1985, when Kasparov defeated him. There followed three further matches against Kasparov, in none of which could Karpov reinstate himself. Then, in 1993, when Kasparov played Short outside FIDE's legislation, FIDE, the World Chess Federation, declared Karpov "World Champion" yet again, after his win against Dutch Grandmaster Jan Timman.

The chess style of Anatoly Karpov lacks the dynamism of Kasparov but his moves are for the connoisseur of gradualism. Karpov has been likened to a poisonous spider, patiently spinning a barely perceptible, yet ultimately lethal web.

Karpov has been declared "World Champion" twice by FIDE, by default. In spite of this somewhat ludicrous state of affairs, we should not let this blind us to the fact that Karpov is a very great player. This he proved by his shattering victory at the Linares tournament of 1994 where he finished ahead, not just of Kasparov but also of Shirov, Anand, Kramnik, Kamsky, Ivanchuk, Gelfand and Polgar, indeed virtually every contender mentioned in this book.

Karpov – Short
Brussels 1987
Queen's Gambit Declined

1   d4   ♘f6

2	c4	e6
3	♘f3	d5
4	♘c3	♗e7
5	♗g5	h6
6	♗xf6	♗xf6
7	e3	0–0
8	♖c1	*(34)*

Karpov adopts what had become Kasparov's favourite method, which he used several times during the 1985 and 1986 world championship matches against Kasparov himself.

8	...	a6
9	a3	c6
10	♗d3	♘d7
11	0–0	b5
12	cxd5	cxd5
13	♘e2	*(35)*

Karpov tries to improve on

the game Portisch – Short, Brussels 1986 where 13 ♘b1 ♗b7 14 a4 bxa4 simply led to a speedy draw. Karpov's choice maintains the tension and avoids premature simplification.

13	...	♗b7
14	♗b1	♖e8
15	♕d3	g6
16	♖fe1	♖c8
17	♖xc8	♕xc8
18	h4	e5 *(36)*

This accepts the liability of an isolated queen's pawn, but Nigel has seen that he can liquidate it fairly quickly.

19	dxe5	♘xe5
20	♘xe5	♖xe5
21	♘f4	d4
22	♕xd4	♕c6
23	e4	♖c5
24	♕e3	♗xh4
25	♘d3	♖h5
26	♗a2	♗d8
27	♘f4	♖g5
28	♗d5	♕c8
29	♗xb7	♕xb7
30	♘d5	*(37)*

White enjoys a slight advantage of superior centralization but this is the kind of position one has to be able to defend if one is to be successful in an extended match against Karpov.

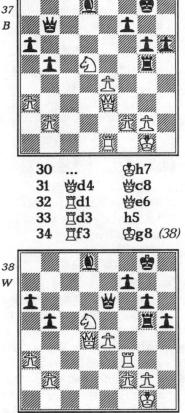

37
B

30	...	♔h7
31	♕d4	♕c8
32	♖d1	♕e6
33	♖d3	h5
34	♖f3	♔g8 *(38)*

38
W

I was watching this game as it was played and here Karpov almost fell into a trap of his own making. Karpov picked up his rook and started to move it towards f6. He knew that 35 ♖f6 ♗xf6 36 ♘xf6+ would lead to a forced win for White, but then he suddenly noticed that 35 ♖f6 would be brutally punished by the intermezzo 35 ...

♖xd5. For an instant Karpov's hand hovered over the board, holding the rook, and then he quickly put this piece down on d3.

35	♖d3	♔h7
36	♖f3	♔g8
37	♔f1	♖e5
38	♖e3	♕d6
39	f4	♖e8
40	e5	♕e6
41	♔g1	♕g4
42	♔h2	♗h4
43	♖f3	*(39)*

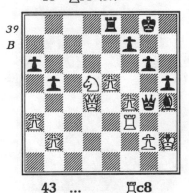

39
B

| 43 | ... | ♖c8 |

Nigel cracks under the constant pressure. 43 ... ♖d8 is forced.

44 ♘e3

Black resigned, since 44 ... ♕e6 45 f5 wins a piece for White.

Karpov – J. Polgar
Monaco 1992
King's Indian Defence

1	c4	g6
2	d4	♗g7
3	♘c3	♘f6
4	e4	d6

5 f3 0-0

It is possible to attack White's centre by playing c5 at once but after 5 ... c5 6 dxc5 dxc5 7 ♕xd8+ ♔xd8 8 ♗e3 Black's position has no dynamism, and, as even the great Bobby Fischer once had to admit, Black can generate no winning chances from this barren wilderness. Indeed, it is Black who has to defend carefully because of the misplaced position of his king.

6 ♗e3 c5 (40)

Interestingly, this thrust makes more sense as a pawn sacrifice since, in order to accept it White has to activate Black's king's rook which now plays an important part in proceedings.

7 dxc5 dxc5
8 ♕xd8 ♖xd8
9 ♗xc5 ♘c6
10 ♘d5 (41)

A natural enough move, though 10 ♗a3 has recently proved more popular, if less effective. For example, in Ivanchuk - Gelfand, Reggio Emilia

1992, Black equalized after 10 ♗a3 e6 11 ♘ge2 b6 12 ♘a4 ♗h6 13 ♖d1 ♗a6 14 ♘ec3 ♘d4 15 ♗d3 ♘h5 (see also Kramnik - Nunn in the section on Kramnik).

10 ... ♘d7

If 10 ... ♘xd5 11 cxd5 ♗xb2 12 ♖d1 and White wins a pawn for no compensation.

11 ♗xe7

If 11 ♘xe7+ ♘xe7 12 ♗xe7 ♗xb2 13 ♗xd8 ♗xa1 and White's development is too retarded and his pawns too scattered to be able to speak of any advantage. The capture with the bishop on move 11 gives up a useful piece but has the virtue of maintaining White's structure intact and of retaining the useful knight on the dominating d5-square.

11 ... ♘xe7
12 ♘xe7+ ♔f8
13 ♘d5 ♗xb2
14 ♖b1 ♗a3
15 ♘h3 b6
16 ♗e2 ♘e5
17 ♘f2 ♗b7
18 f4 ♘c6
19 h4

Partly to generate counter-play by advancing the pawn and partly to develop his rook via h3.

19	...	♘d4
20	♖h3	♖ac8
21	h5 *(42)*	

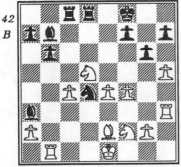

Black clearly has superb positional compensation for the sacrificed pawn in terms of superior coordination. White obviously cannot play 21 ♖xa3 on account of 21 ... ♘c2+. Even after the text Black has adequate counterplay.

| 21 | ... | ♗xd5 |
| 22 | cxd5 | ♖c2 |

At this point the 15 year old Hungarian teenage girl prodigy overplays her hand. Simpler would have been 22 ... ♘xe2 23 ♔xe2 ♖c2+ or 22 ... ♘xe2 23 ♖xa3 ♘xf4 when Black is in no danger. After the text her pieces get into something of a tangle and Karpov does what he is best at doing, namely consolidation.

23	♗d3	♖xa2
24	♗c4	♖c2
25	♖xa3	♖xc4

26 ♖xa7

Suddenly White has the advantage again. Karpov is still a pawn up, he has a rook on the 7th, Black's b-pawn is weak, White's centre is secure (the knight on f2 is a brilliant defender) and even White's h-pawn has something to say in the future.

26	...	b5
27	h6	b4
28	♘g4	♘c2+
29	♔d2	♘a3
30	♖f1 *(43)*	

Karpov has seen that he does not need to defend his e-pawn.

| 30 | ... | ♖xe4 |
| 31 | ♘f6 | |

This is decisive since Black can no longer defend the pawn on h7, after which White's h6-pawn becomes a mighty force.

31	...	♖d4+
32	♔e3	♘c2+
33	♔f3	♖d3+
34	♔e2	♖3xd5

Vainly hoping that White will be distracted by the

meagre booty of 35 ♘xd5, but first Karpov introduces an important intermezzo.

35 ♘xh7+ *(44)*

44 B

The rook cannot run away.

35	...	♔g8
36	♘f6+	♔h8
37	♘xd5	♖xd5
38	♖xf7	b3
39	♖b7	♘d4+
40	♔f2	♘b5
41	♖a1	♖d2+
42	♔g3	♖a2
43	♖d1	**Black resigns**

Karpov holds the world record for victories in first class tournaments, now over one hundred. Here is an example.

Dortmund 1993

Karpov 5½/7; Kramnik, Lutz 4; Kamsky, Dolmatov 3½; Lautier 3; Serper 2½; Lobron 2.

Kamsky – Karpov
Dortmund 1993

45 B

This is a well-known position from the Caro-Kann, an opening Karpov has recently honed into a most resilient, forceful weapon. Karpov's next move is entirely new and totally unexpected. It shows a kind of freedom of thought one associates with Capablanca. Most people, even if they had thought of the move, would probably not have had the courage to play it, in view of the chances White obtains by sacrificing a pawn.

11 ... ♔e7

Black's staggering threat is 12 ... g5 trapping White's queen. White has to perform contortions to avoid this. The chief point of 11 ... ♔e7 was to defend Black's king's rook to facilitate the threat of ... g5.

12 ♘e5

Sacrificing a pawn. The alternative is 12 ♗f4 ♗b4+ 13 ♗d2 ♗xd2+ 14 ♔xd2 with approximate equality. After 12 ♗f4 g5 would fail to 13 ♗xd6+ ♛xd6 14 ♘xg5.

12	...	♗xe5
13	dxe5	♛a5+
14	c3	♛xe5+

Black's capture of the gambit pawn looks risky, but White never gets his queen into the attack.

15	♗e3	b6
16	0-0-0	g5
17	♛a4	c5
18	♖he1	♗d7
19	♛a3	♖hd8
20	g3	♛c7
21	♗d4	♗e8
22	♔b1	♖d5
23	f4	♖ad8 (46)

White is still struggling to introduce his queen into the game. Meanwhile, Karpov organises a mass exchange of rooks to stress the importance of his extra pawn.

24	♗c2	♖5d6
25	♗xf6+	♔xf6
26	fxg5+	hxg5
27	♖xd6	♖xd6
28	c4	♔e7

White's next, resurrecting his queen, keeps his prospects alive.

29	♛e3	f6
30	h4	gxh4
31	gxh4	

At last Kamsky has chances with his outside passed pawn.

31	...	♛d7
32	♛h6	e5
33	h5	♛g4
34	♛h7+	♔d8
35	h6	♖d2 (47)

This part of the game looks as if it was played in a mutual time scramble. The threat of ... ♖xc2 followed by ... ♗g6 bluffs White into exchanging queens when, in fact, 36 ♛xa7 would still have left matters entirely unclear.

36	♛f5	♛xf5
37	♗xf5	♗d7
38	♗g6	♖h2

Now it is easy. Black's rook controls White's passed pawn while White has no defence to Black's rumbling army in the centre.

39	h7	♔e7
40	♗d3	♗e6
41	♖g1	f5
42	♖g7+	♔f6

43	♖xa7	e4
44	♗e2	f4
45	b3	f3
46	♘d1	♗f5
47	♔c1	♗xh7
48	♖b7	♔e5
49	♖xb6	♖xa2

White resigns

While the real 1993 world championship match was being played in London between World Champion Kasparov and and his Challenger, Nigel Short, the FIDE (World Chess Federation) version, between Jan Timman of Holland and the former world champion Anatoly Karpov of Russia was stumbling along in the background. That match started, much as it was to continue, with the stage set spectacularly bursting into flames during the opening speeches before the first game in Zwolle. In spite of the fact that a Dutch hero was participating, the Dutch portion had to be divided up between three Dutch cities and not one single guilder was raised in prize money. At the midway stage the FIDE contest suffered a calamity, when the Sultanate of Oman (which had originally promised to host the second half) withdrew their offer. There was an embarrassing hiatus, while Campomanes, the FIDE president, tried to hawk his second hand chess match around the globe. Fi-

nally, Djakarta took the bait, though it is still unclear, even though the match has long been finished, how much prize money was at stake, or simply the empty title of FIDE champion. The games from Holland, although hardly worthy of a world championship contest, did exhibit some points of interest. At least, that was until Timman realized that the Omanis had withdrawn, when game 11 ended as a draw after just a few moves with no pieces having been exchanged. Clearly, at that moment, the players had gone on strike. In contrast, the games in Djakarta, though hard fought, were, frankly, an embarrassment. They were literally full of errors that even club standard players would have avoided.

**Karpov – Timman
FIDE World Championship,
Game 14,
Djakarta 1993**

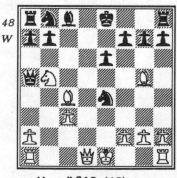

48
W

11   ♗f4? *(48)*

A new move and a bad one. 11 ♕d4 had led to a quick draw in game eight. Karpov's attempt to improve should have been disastrous.

11	...	0–0
12	0–0	♘d7
13	♘c7	e5
14	♘xa8	exf4
15	♗d5	♘df6

Black could win with 15 ... ♘ef6 16 ♗f3 ♘e5 17 ♖e1 ♕xc3 or 17 ♕d6 ♘xf3+ 18 gxf3 ♗h3.

| 16 | ♗xe4 | ♘xe4 |
| 17 | f3 | (49) |

| 17 | ... | ♘xc3?? |

Black could still win with 17 ... ♖d8, e.g. 18 ♕e2 ♕c5+ 19 ♔h1 ♘g3+ 20 hxg3 ♕h5+ 21 ♔g1 fxg3 or 18 ♕e1 ♕c5+ 19 ♔h1 ♘f6 when White's errant knight on a8 is trapped and Black will win on material.

| 18 | ♕d6 | |

Now White's knight escapes.

18	...	♘d5
19	♖ac1	♗e6
20	♘c7	♘xc7
21	♕xc7	♕xc7
22	♖xc7	♗d5
23	♖c5	♗e6

24	♖c7	♗d5
25	♖c5	♗e6
26	♖a5	a6
27	♖b1	♖c8 (50)

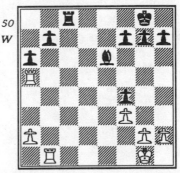

After a comedy of errors, Karpov has finally emerged with the advantage and went on to win competently after a further twenty or so moves.

Demoralized by this defeat Timman handled game 15 like a beginner.

**Timman – Karpov
FIDE World Championship,
Game 15,
Djakarta 1993
Nimzo–Indian Defence**

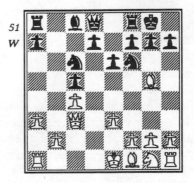

10 ♘h3?

He has to play 10 ♗d3.

10 ...   h6

11 ♗h4??

A dreadful move, which allows White's king to be displaced for no compensation. White must play 11 ♗xf6!.

11 ...   g5
12 ♗g3   ♘e4
13 ♕c2   ♕a5+
14 ♔e2   f5
15 f3   ♘xg3+
16 hxg3   ♖b8
17 ♘f2   ♗a6
18 ♘d3   d5
19 b3   ♖xb3

This sacrifice is decisive.

20 ♕xb3   dxc4
21 ♕a2   cxd3+
22 ♔f2   ♖f6
23 ♖c1   ♔g7
24 f4   c4
25 ♕b2   e5

Timman is overwhelmed by the hoard of black pawns.

26 fxg5   hxg5
27 ♖c3   ♕b6
28 ♕xb6   axb6
29 ♖h5   ♘e7
30 ♗xd3   cxd3
31 ♖c7   ♖e6
32 ♔e1   ♗b5
33 g4   ♔g6
34 ♖h8   f4

White resigns

Linares 1994

		1	2	3	4	5	6	7	8	9	0	1	2	3	4	
1	Karpov	*	½	½	1	1	1	½	½	1	1	1	1	1	1	11
2	Shirov	½	*	½	0	1	0	½	1	1	1	½	1	1	½	8½
3	Kasparov	½	½	*	1	0	0	1	1	½	1	½	1	1	½	8½
4	Bareev	0	1	0	*	½	½	½	½	1	1	0	1	½	1	7½
5	Kramnik	0	0	1	½	*	½	½	½	0	½	½	1	1	1	7
6	Lautier	0	1	1	½	½	*	1	0	1	0	½	0	1	½	7
7	Anand	½	½	0	½	½	0	*	1	0	0	½	1	1	1	6½
8	Kamsky	½	0	0	½	½	1	0	*	½	½	½	1	½	1	6½
9	Topalov	0	0	½	0	1	0	1	½	*	1	1	½	0	1	6½
10	Ivanchuk	0	0	0	0	½	1	1	½	0	*	½	1	½	1	6
11	Gelfand	0	½	½	1	½	½	½	½	0	½	*	0	½	½	5½
12	Illescas	0	0	0	0	0	1	0	0	½	0	1	*	1	1	4½
13	Polgar	0	0	0	½	0	0	0	½	1	½	½	0	*	1	4
14	Beliavsky	0	½	½	0	0	½	0	0	0	0	½	0	0	*	2

Karpov's result at Linares has fuelled considerable speculation as to whether it was the greatest single tournament performance of all time. Two other competitions, San Remo 1930, dominated by Alekhine and the US Championship of 1963/64, won by Fischer with a 100% score, also come into contention for this particular laurel.

Alekhine's result came against the greatest players of his day apart from Lasker and Capablanca. But it should be noted that many of Alekhine's opponents, although rated the world's best at that time were ageing grandmasters not far from retirement. The new generation of Euwe, Botvinnik, Keres, Reshevsky and Fine was on the horizon but had not yet made their mark.

Fischer's performance came only in a national championship, but a particularly strong one which included no less than three players (Benko, Byrne and Reshevsky) who have competed at Candidates level. With many other competent grandmasters in the field, this result was truly staggering.

The only top men missing from Linares were Short and Adams. I would rate Karpov's performance as better than Alekhine's but I still find Fischer's 100% miraculous.

Kevin O'Connell, one of the world's leading rating experts, has calculated the top ten tournament rating performances of all time.

	Player	Event	Rating
1	Fischer	US Championship 1964	3000+
2	Karpov	Linares 1994	2977
3	Kasparov	Tilburg 1989	2913
4	Alekhine	San Remo 1930	2906
5	Kasparov	Linares 1993	2879
	Zsofia Polgar	Rome 1989	2879
7	Kasparov	Linares 1992	2866
8	Botvinnik	Hague, Moscow 1948	2822
	Lasker	St Petersburg 1914	2822
10	Nunn	Olympiad 1984	2810

Karpov – Topalov
Linares 1994
English Opening

1 d4   ♘f6
2 c4   c5
3 ♘f3

Karpov has never been comfortable against the Benko Gambit which occurs after 3 d5 b5, hence this more strategic selection.

3 ...   cxd4
4 ♘xd4   e6

It would have been interesting to see how Karpov would have reacted to another gambit, 4 ... e5 5 ♘b5 d5 6 cxd5 ♗c5, which Kasparov has occasionally employed to good effect.

5 g3   ♘c6

6	♗g2	♗c5
7	♘b3	♗e7
8	♘c3	0-0
9	0-0	d6
10	♗f4	

The routine move would be 10 e4 but then, by means of ... a6 followed by ... ♕c7 Black could enter a standard and resilient Hedgehog-type set-up. Karpov's choice is superior in that, while refusing to occupy the centre with his e-pawn, he maintains his fianchettoed king's bishop on a vigorous open diagonal.

10	...	♘h5
11	e3	

This is a startling concept. Karpov surrenders the bishop pair and accepts doubled pawns, but, in return for infringing such elementary strategic principles, he gains open lines, particularly the e-file, while vastly increasing his command of the light squares. The more stereotyped 11 ♗e3 was played in the game Mikhalchishin-Kasparov, Baku 1980.

11	...	♘xf4
12	exf4	♗d7
13	♕d2	♕b8
14	♖fe1	

Already threatening 15 f5, to undermine Black's central bastions.

14	...	g6

For the moment stopping the threat, but now White has a further target for operations on the king's flank.

15	h4	a6

The apparently more natural 15 ... h5 would fail to 16 f5 exf5 17 ♗xc6 ♗xc6 18 ♖xe7 winning, or 16 f5 gxf5 17 ♕h6 with devastation in the black king's field.

16	h5	b5

Black is dicing with death. This premature thrust accentuates the pressure from White's bishop on g2 and permits Karpov to exploit the undefended situation of Black's bishop on d7. Surely the patient 16 ... ♖d8 followed, if necessary, by the defensively retrograde manoeuvre ... ♗e8, to shore up his king's defences, would have been more prudent.

17	hxg6	hxg6
18	♘c5	

A rude awakening for Black. From here to the end of the game the Bulgarian grandmaster is given no respite whatsoever.

18	...	dxc5

If 18 ... ♗e8 19 ♘xa6! ♖xa6 20 cxb5 wins, so 18 ... dxc5 is forced.

19	♕xd7	♖c8

An ingenious defence, but one which Karpov swiftly reveals as a purely temporary expedient. Topalov hopes for 20 ♗xc6 when 20 ... ♖a7 would repel boarders without serious loss. Instead Karpov launches a raid from an entirely different direction.

20	♖xe6	(52)

A brilliant irruption. It makes

no difference whether Black immediately captures the rook or first prods the white queen.

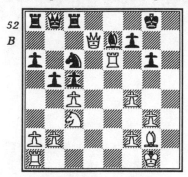

52
B

| 20 | ... | ♖a7 |
| 21 | ♖xg6+ |

Karpov insists on his sacrifice. Black must accept for if 21 ... ♔f8 22 ♕h3 fxg6 23 ♕h8+ or 21 ... ♔h7 22 ♕h3+ ♔xg6 23 ♗e4+ with a winning attack.

21	...	fxg6
22	♕e6+	♔g7
23	♗xc6	♖d8
24	cxb5

White's combination is over. With three pawns for the exchange and Black's king's fortress in ruins, Karpov has an easily won position.

24	...	♗f6
25	♘e4	♗d4
26	bxa6	♕b6
27	♖d1	♕xa6
28	♖xd4	*(53)*

A final sacrifice which abolishes Black's vestigial resistance on the dark squares.

53
B

28	...	♖xd4
29	♕f6+	♔g8
30	♕xg6+	♔f8
31	♕e8+	♔g7
32	♕e5+	♔g8
33	♘f6+	♔f7
34	♗e8+	♔f8
35	♕xc5+

In the long run, it was inevitable that this check would regain most of the sacrificed material. If now 35 ... ♖d6 36 ♘e4 wins easily enough.

35	...	♕d6
36	♕xa7	♕xf6
37	♗h5	♖d2
38	b3	♖b2
39	♔g2

Black resigns

Black has had enough. There is no vulnerable point in White's camp and Black can scarcely move a piece without shedding further material or permitting the decisive advance of White's army of queenside pawns.

3   Bobby Fischer - The King Over the Water

Player's Name: Bobby Fischer
Date of Birth: 9 March 1943
Nationality: USA
Main Strengths
Brilliant attacker, uncompromising in quest for victory, even in level positions.
Main Weaknesses
Rusty opening theory; no longer relishes defence.

Before departing from the 1993 Championship in London, Kasparov lambasted the role of the KGB in seeking to determine the results of past world title matches in favour of the darlings of the Soviet establishment. Kasparov said: "The KGB was capable of anything if they were in search of a result that suited them." Indeed, in the wake of the collapse of the Soviet Empire, widespread evidence is emerging, from newly released documents, of activities undertaken by the KGB and the Soviet Propaganda Ministry against both great chess champions, Bobby Fischer and Garry Kasparov. One key new text is a manuscript, hitherto unpublished in the west, entitled *Russians versus Fischer*. It is introduced by grand-master Yuri Averbakh, arbiter for *The Times* World Chess Championship. Averbakh was a chess champion in Stalin's USSR of the 1950s. The book publishes secret documents that reveal how the KGB blocked the path of Bobby Fischer.

I well recall the grip that Soviet officialdom still exerted in its declining years over even the greatest of world chess champions. At the Seville championship of 1987, when Kasparov narrowly retained his title against Anatoly Karpov, the brilliant and popular former world champion Mikhail Tal had been invited by the Spanish organisers as a commentator for the public. Tal, however, made one unfortunate mistake; he was overly critical of Karpov's play. Karpov was the favourite of the Soviet chess establishment which still hoped, in vain as it turned out, that Karpov would unseat the unruly Kasparov as world champion. Official retribution from Moscow was swift for Tal's indiscretion. His travel permits were withdrawn and he was summarily ordered back to Moscow, well before the period of his invitation had expired. It was humiliating that so great a figure should have been exposed as a helpless pawn in the hands of faceless Soviet functionaries.

In 1972, Fischer had defeated Boris Spassky, to take the world title in a chess match which symbolised the cold war itself between the USSR and the USA. Three years later Fischer had to defend his title against Anatoly Karpov. The American demanded new conditions for a title defence, namely that the championship would go to the first man to win ten games, with the champion retaining his title in the event of a 9–9 score. The Soviets were quick and merciless in opposing these conditions, clearly having in mind the scenario, which turned out to be correct, that Fischer would default the match, rather than give in, and abandon his new conditions.

The most fascinating section of *Russians versus Fischer* is titled "The match that never was – secret documents of the Central Committee of the Communist Party". There Viktor Korchnoi is quoted: "The genius Fischer was not given the chance to defend his title ... what followed was that the Soviets later adopted Fischer's idea of an open ended match ... but instead of the two point handicap they protected the new Soviet world champion Karpov far more reliably and far more ruthlessly – by insisting on a return match." Grandmaster Lev Alburt is also cited: "Everything did end in a fracas. Fischer was incensed by FIDE's rejection of his proposal that in the event of a 9–9 score the champion should retain his title. The World Chess Federation (FIDE) clearly supported the Soviet challenger. It is interesting that Karpov, on becoming champion, went on to secure much greater privileges for himself."

One game which the KGB did not need to influence was the following, one of the most brilliant draws on record.

Fischer – Tal
Leipzig Olympiad 1960
French Defence

1	e4	e6
2	d4	d5
3	♘c3	♗b4

4	e5	c5
5	a3	♗a5
6	b4	cxd4
7	♕g4	♘e7
8	bxa5	dxc3
9	♕xg7	♖g8
10	♕xh7	♘bc6
11	♘f3	♕c7
12	♗b5	♗d7
13	0-0	0-0-0
14	♗g5 *(54)*	

54
B

Black's next move sets off a dazzling series of fireworks. Fischer had at first assumed that Tal was merely trying to confuse the issue.

14	...	♘xe5
15	♘xe5	♗xb5
16	♘xf7	♗xf1
17	♘xd8	♖xg5
18	♘xe6	♖xg2+ *(55)*

55
W

| 19 | ♔h1 | |

The saving move for White. If 19 ♔xf1 ♖xh2 20 ♕f7 (20 ♘xc7 ♖xh7 wins a piece) 20 ... ♖h1+ produces a winning attack.

19	...	♕e5
20	♖xf1	♕xe6
21	♔xg2	♕g4+
	Draw	

US Championship 1963/64

		1	2	3	4	5	6	7	8	9	0	1	2	
1	Fischer	*	1	1	1	1	1	1	1	1	1	1	1	11
2	Evans	0	*	1	½	½	½	0	1	1	1	1	1	7½
3	Benko	0	0	*	1	½	1	1	1	½	1	½	½	7
4	Saidy	0	½	0	*	0	½	1	1	1	1	½	1	6½
5	Reshevsky	0	½	½	1	*	½	0	½	1	1	1	½	6½
6	Byrne R	0	½	0	½	½	*	0	½	1	1	1	½	5½
7	Weinstein	0	1	0	0	1	1	*	0	0	0	1	1	5
8	Bisguier	0	0	0	0	½	½	1	*	1	0	½	1	4½
9	Addison	0	0	½	0	0	0	1	0	*	½	½	1	3½
10	Mednis	0	0	0	0	0	0	1	1	½	*	½	½	3½
11	Steinmeyer	0	0	½	½	0	0	0	½	½	½	*	½	3
12	Byrne D	0	0	½	0	½	½	0	0	0	½	½	*	2½

In the 1964 US Championship Fischer scored 100% against a Grandmaster field, perhaps the single most remarkable tournament performance in the history of chess.

Boris Spassky, who seized the world title from Tigran Petrosian at Moscow in 1969, was an adventurous attacker. His play was very much in the mould of Tal and Alekhine, yet in Fischer he succumbed to the prophet of heroic materialism. Fischer was a chess superman who would snatch material, in a fashion that might have seemed sordid in a lesser player, only to release it at the appropriate moment for overwhelming advantages in terms of the initiative, mobility and striking power. It was a tragedy for the world of chess that Fischer did not play a single serious tournament or match game for the two decades from 1972 to 1992.

One of Fischer's masterpieces from his conquest of the supreme title in 1972:

**Fischer – Spassky
World Championship,
Game 10, Reykjavik 1972
Ruy Lopez**

1	e4	e5
2	♘f3	♘c6
3	♗b5	a6
4	♗a4	♘f6
5	0-0	♗e7
6	♖e1	b5
7	♗b3	d6
8	c3	0-0
9	h3	♘b8 (56)

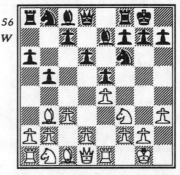

The so-called Breyer Variation. It is apparently time-wasting but difficult to break down.

10	d4	♘bd7
11	♘bd2	♗b7
12	♗c2	♖e8
13	b4	♗f8
14	a4	♘b6
15	a5	♘bd7
16	♗b2	♕b8

Later it was discovered that Black could improve his play considerably with 16 ... ♖b8 17 ♖b1 ♗a8 18 ♗a1 h6 19 dxe5 dxe5 20 c4 c5 21 cxb5 axb5 22 ♕e2 Hjartarson – Beliavsky, Belfort World Cup 1988.

17 ♖b1

White's idea is to play c4, opening up the game with White's rook staring uncomfortably at the black queen on the same file.

| 17 | ... | c5 |
| 18 | bxc5 | dxc5 |

19	dxe5	♘xe5
20	♘xe5	♛xe5
21	c4	♛f4
22	♗xf6	(57)

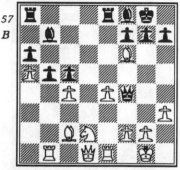

57
B

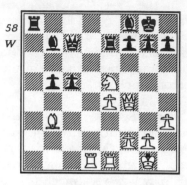

58
W

30	♗xf7+	♖xf7
31	♛xf7+	♛xf7
32	♘xf7	♗xe4

22	...	♛xf6

Sammy Reshevsky suggested the somewhat paradoxical 22 ... gxf6 in order to retain the queen in its strong outpost position. Black's further plan would be to mobilise swiftly with ... ♖ad8 and ... ♗h6.

23	cxb5	♖ed8
24	♛c1	♛c3

24 ... axb5 would have been safer.

25	♘f3	♛xa5
26	♗b3	

All the action appears so far to have been on the queenside but this superb move puts the finger on Black's main weakness – the pawn at f7.

26	...	axb5
27	♛f4	♖d7
28	♘e5	♛c7
29	♖bd1	♖e7 (58)

29 ... ♖xd1 is met by 30 ♗xf7+ ♔h8 31 ♘g6+ and mate next move. Therefore White wins material.

Black loses without a fight after 32 ... ♔xf7 33 ♖d7+. In the endgame which follows Fischer has the advantage of rook for bishop but must still cope with the problem of Black's connected passed pawns on the queenside. The key to Fischer's success is his ability to paralyse Black's passed pawns while gradually mobilising his own majority of pawns on the other side of the board.

33	♖xe4	♗xf7
34	♖d7+	♔f6
35	♖b7	♖a1+
36	♔h2	♗d6+
37	g3	b4
38	♔g2	h5
39	♖b6	♖d1
40	♔f3	♔f7
41	♔e2	♖d5
42	f4	g6
43	g4	hxg4
44	hxg4	g5
45	f5	♗e5
46	♖b5	♔f6 (59)

59
W

If 46 ... ♘d4 then 47 ♖e6
threatening ♖g6. The rest is a

demonstration of Fischer's
admirable technique.

47	♖exb4	♘d4
48	♖b6+	♔e5
49	♔f3	♖d8
50	♖b8	♖d7
51	♖4b7	♖d6
52	♖b6	♖d7
53	♖g6	♔d5
54	♖xg5	♘e5
55	f6	♔d4
56	♖b1	

Black resigns

World Championship, Reykjavik 1972

	1	2	3	4	5	6	7	8	9	10	11
Fischer	0	0	1	½	1	1	½	1	½	1	0
Spassky	1	1	0	½	0	0	½	0	½	0	1

	12	13	14	15	16	17	18	19	20	21	
Fischer	½	1	½	½	½	½	½	½	½	1	12½
Spassky	½	0	½	½	½	½	½	½	½	0	8½

After Bobby Fischer had defaulted his world championship title in 1975, and Anatoly Karpov had become world champion, without playing a match, efforts were still made to revive the Karpov - Fischer championship, a match which Fischer deserved and which the whole chess world wanted to see. However, as *Russians versus Fischer* proves, this was opposed and frustrated at the highest level of Soviet officialdom. The authors quote secret letter number 3403C, October 20th 1976: "'The USSR Sports Committee continues to con-

sider it inexpedient in principle for such a match to be held. Should Fischer and his associates propose specific conditions, we regard it as expedient to drag out the talks and work out counter-proposals that would be unacceptable to R. Fischer.' This decision bore the signature of Politburo Member M. Suslov, the country's chief ideologue." Further documents by G. Smirnov, Deputy Head of the Propaganda Department, and M. Zimianin and K. Katushev, both Central Committee Secretaries, support this view (Secret Memo to the Central

Committee of the Communist Party number 2791C, August 11th 1976). Kremlin 1 - Fischer 0!!

Fischer's Comeback

No-one had believed that it could possibly happen. After two decades in the wilderness, the mercurial American genius, Bobby Fischer, made a come-back. For twenty years, after decisively beating Soviet World Champion Boris Spassky in the most celebrated chess match of all time at Reykjavik in 1972, Fischer did not play a single game of match or tournament chess.

The play in their rematch was a mixture of brilliance and blunders. By general consent the first game was a true Fischer masterpiece, which astounded experts and grand-masters alike. It seemed that Fischer's absence for twenty years from the chessboard had in no way blunted the ferocity of his mental cutting edge. Even better was to come, in the shape of game 11. This was a game where Spassky defended tenaciously and ingeniously, yet was bowled over by the dazzl-ing force of Fischer's attack.

Punctuating such master-pieces were the horrors of games 5 and 19, where Fischer drifted planlessly. These were games scarcely to be distinguished from those of amateur level. World Champion Garry Kasparov dismissed all the games as inferior and not up to championship standard but, to quote Mandy Rice-Davies, "He would, wouldn't he?". Fischer is the only Cham-pion in the 100 plus years of the official Championship who can seriously challenge Kaspa-rov's position as the strongest and most highly-rated player of all time. These two are the pinnacle of chess. On paper, Kasparov's rating is the higher; yet it is Fischer who has estab-lished himself as the greatest personality amongst the public at large.

Now that Fischer has over-come Spassky for the second time, will he go back to sulk in his Pasadena tent for another twenty years? Alternatively, will his sanction-busting activi-ties, playing in Belgrade in defiance of UN sanctions, even permit him to re-enter the United States? It is possible that he might stay in Belgrade, move to Budapest, or even join Boris Spassky in exile in Paris.

The only satisfactory out-come for the chess world is for Fischer now to take on a su-perior opponent to Boris Spassky, one who will really test him, preferably Nigel Short. Ultimately, a Fischer - Kasparov match would resolve the question of who is the greatest warrior of the mind on the planet.

The moves alone cannot do justice to what was, by general consent, the most brilliant game of the match. Game 11 was fully the equal of, if not better than any of their games from Reykjavik 1972. It featured an unusual and original opening by Fischer, a new pawn sacrifice which overturns established theory in the chosen line, a scintillating attack, full of neat points, matched by robust and highly imaginative defence from Spassky. The whole creation was topped off with some very neat points in the endgame. This was a true masterpiece.

Fischer – Spassky
"World Championship Match", Game 11,
Sveti Stefan 1992
Sicilian Defence

1	e4	c5
2	♘f3	♘c6
3	♗b5	

A rare treatment for Fischer, who habitually preferred the open Sicilian with 3 d4.

| 3 | ... | g6 |
| 4 | ♗xc6 | *(60)* |

And this early exchange of bishop for knight is quite unexpected. Curiously, Fischer seems to have evinced a marked predilection for knights over bishops in this match, a theme which is worth exploring.

An alternative is 4 0-0 ♗g7 5 c3 ♘f6 6 ♖e1 0-0 7 d4 d5! 8 exd5 ♕xd5 with active play for Black in the game Speelman, Keene, King + Forbes v Kasparov and Short, consultation game for TV, London 1993.

| 4 | ... | bxc6 |

It is natural enough to recapture towards the centre while simultaneously giving himself the chance to occupy the b-file with a rook. At this point, though, Spassky should probably have contented himself with the more humble recapture 4 ... dxc6 which would have avoided the troubles to come. To be fair, Fischer's treatment was hard to foresee.

| 5 | 0-0 | ♗g7 |
| 6 | ♖e1 | e5 |

6 ... f6!, as Spassky played in a later game in the match, is better.

| 7 | b4!! | *(61)* |

A brilliant innovation, sacrificing a pawn to gain control of the dark squares. Previous theory recognised only 7 c3 which, in comparison, is relatively harmless.

7	...	cxb4
8	a3	c5

If 8 ... bxa3 White has a pleasant choice between 9 ♘xa3, 9 ♗xa3 or 9 d4 exd4 10 e5 when Black's dark-square situation in the centre is looking perilous.

9	axb4	cxb4
10	d4	exd4 (62)

11 ♗b2

Also attractive is 11 e5 but Fischer has foreseen that Black has grave problems along the dark-squared diagonal a1-h8.

11	...	d6
12	♘xd4	♕d7

If 12 ... ♘e7 13 ♘c6 ♘xc6 14 ♗xg7 gives White more than enough compensation in terms

of dark-square domination.

13 ♘d2 (63)

13 ... ♗b7

If instead 13 ... ♘e7 14 ♘c4 ♗b7 15 ♘e6!! when White wins spectacularly in every variation.

14 ♘c4 ♘h6

14 ... ♘e7 again fails to 15 ♘e6!! while 14 ... ♔f8 loses attractively to 15 e5 dxe5 16 ♘xe5 ♕d5 (16 ... ♗xe5 17 ♖xe5 is too horrible to contemplate) 17 ♘d7+ ♕xd7 18 ♘e6+ and Black can resign.

15 ♘f5!! (64)

A superb move which devastates Black's position and much superior to 15 ♘b5 ♗xb2 16 ♘bxd6+ when 16 ... ♔e7 attacks the white knight. Since now 15 ... ♘xf5 16 exf5 is discovered check, Spassky must fall in with Fischer's plans.

15	...	♗xb2
16	♘cxd6+	♔f8
17	♘xh6	f6 *(65)*

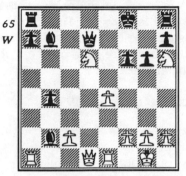

17 ... ♗xa1 18 ♕xa1 ♕xd6 19 ♕xh8+ grants White a raging attack. Meanwhile, the threat of either ♘xf7 forces Black to lose the exchange in this fashion.

18	♘df7	♕xd1
19	♖axd1	♔e7
20	♘xh8	♖xh8 *(66)*

Black has lost the exchange but still has fighting chances due to his passed a-pawn and the bishop pair. However, Fischer now has a fabulous

solution available, very much like a conjuror producing a rabbit out of a hat, which dispels any illusion that Black can survive.

| 21 | ♘f5+!! | gxf5 |
| 22 | exf5+ | ♗e5 |

He must give back the material. 22 ... ♔f8 23 ♖d8+ is obviously hopeless.

23	f4	♖c8
24	fxe5	♖xc2
25	e6	♗c6

And not 25 ... ♖xg2+ 26 ♔f1 ♗c6 27 ♖d7+ ♗xd7 28 exd7+ ♔xd7 29 ♔xg2 winning.

26	♖c1	♖xc1
27	♖xc1	♔d6
28	♖d1+	♔e5

If 28 ... ♔e7 29 ♖a1 wins.

| 29 | e7 | a5 *(67)* |

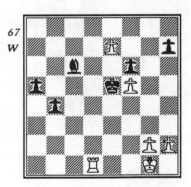

Black's pawns are not fast enough.

30	♖c1	♗d7
31	♖c5+	♔d4
32	♖xa5	b3
33	♖a7	♗e8
34	♖b7	♔c3
35	♔f2	b2
36	♔e3	♗f7

36 ... ♔c2 37 ♔d4 makes no difference.

37	g4	♔c2
38	♔d4	b1♕
39	♖xb1	♔xb1
40	♔c5	♔c2
41	♔d6	

Black resigns

The final position is an easy win for White. For example 41 ... ♔d3 42 ♔d7 ♔e4 43 e8♕+ ♘xe8+ 44 ♔xe8 ♔f4 45 ♔f7 ♔g5 46 h4+ ♔xh4 47 ♔xf6 ♔xg4 48 ♔e6 h5 49 f6 h4 50 f7 h3 51 f8♕ h2 52 ♕f1 and the game is up.

Everyone in the chess world would love to see Fischer play again. The two games we have just seen were superb jewels of the intellect.

"World Championship", Sveti Stefan/Belgrade 1992

	1	*2*	*3*	*4*	*5*	*6*	*7*	*8*	*9*	*10*	
Fischer	1	½	½	0	0	½	1	1	1	½	
Spassky	0	½	½	1	1	½	0	0	0	½	

	11	*12*	*13*	*14*	*15*	*16*	*17*	*18*	*19*	*20*	
Fischer	1	0	½	½	½	1	1	½	½	0	
Spassky	0	1	½	½	½	0	0	½	½	1	

	21	*22*	*23*	*24*	*25*	*26*	*27*	*28*	*29*	*30*	
Fischer	1	½	½	½	1	0	½	½	½	1	17½
Spassky	0	½	½	½	0	1	½	½	½	0	12½

4 Nigel Short

Player's Name: Nigel Short
Date of Birth: 1 June 1965
Nationality: British
Main Strengths
Exceedingly dangerous attacking player after 1 e4. Particular expert in the Sicilian and Ruy Lopez.
Main Weaknesses
Vulnerable as Black against top opposition; lacks fully viable repertoire against 1 d4.

Nigel Short is the only player in this chapter who has already achieved the glory of contending a world title match. He challenged Kasparov in London 1993. Indeed, he is the first British player since the days of Staunton, in 1843 to achieve such eminence.

The following game is from the only previous match between Short and Kasparov, in which Nigel won two to Kasparov's four, a creditable performance.

**Short – Kasparov
Thames TV Docklands Trophy,
London Hippodrome 1987
Sicilian Defence**

1   e4   c5

2   ♘f3   d6
3   d4   cxd4
4   ♘xd4   ♘f6

The Sicilian is more of a counterattack than a defence. It has a risky reputation, but also scores a high percentage of wins. To Kasparov, it is second nature to play it.

5   ♘c3   a6
6   ♗e3   e6
7   f3   ♘bd7
8   g4   h6
9   h4

In game 2 of this match, Kasparov had continued with 9 ... b5. Now, he comes up with a major improvement.

9   ...   ♘e5
10   ♖g1 *(68)*

Surprised by the innovation, Nigel goes astray. The correct course is 10 ♕e2 planning

0-0-0. After White's error, Garry immediately captures the initiative.

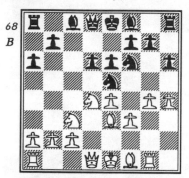

68
B

| 10 | ... | ♛b6 |
| 11 | ♕c1 | d5 |

The correct countermeasure to White's wing manoeuvres. Black strikes back in the centre.

12	♗e2	dxe4
13	♘xe4	♘xe4
14	fxe4	♗e7
15	♖h1	♗d7
16	c3	♛c7
17	♗f2	b5 (69)

69
W

Now Black has the initiative.

| 18 | ♕c2 | ♘c4 |
| 19 | ♗xc4 | ♛xc4 |

Black's 19th move is incorrect. It might have been profitably replaced with 19 ... bxc4 intending to pile up against White's position by later doubling rooks in the open b-file.

20	b3	♛c7
21	0-0-0	0-0
22	♔b1	a5
23	g5	h5
24	♖hg1	a4

The wrong way of prosecuting the assault. More promising would have been the pawn sacrifice 24 ... b4.

25	b4	♖ac8
26	♖d3	g6
27	♗g3	♛b7
28	♕e2	♖c4
29	♗e5 (70)	

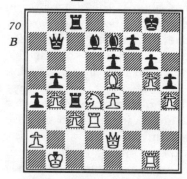

70
B

White's bishop has seized a splendid diagonal.

29	...	♖fc8
30	♕e3	♗c6
31	♖e1	a3
32	♕f2	

It might seem that Kasparov has a devastating sacrificial combination at his fingertips, namely 32 ... ♘xb4 33 cxb4 ♗xe4 34 ♖xe4 ♛xe4 35 ♕xe4 ♖c1 checkmate.

However, the interpolation 33 ♕f6! foils all of this ingenuity and leaves Black himself facing checkmate.

32	...	♗e8
33	♘b3	♕c6
34	♘a5	♖xb4+ *(71)*

71
W

White appears to be crushed, since 35 cxb4 permits ... ♕c2+. But Nigel has seen further than the world champion.

| 35 | ♔a1!! | |

This cool retreat into the corner leaves Black with his queen and rook under attack. Kasparov tries some ingenious last-minute sacrifices.

35	...	♕c5
36	cxb4	♕xb4
37	♕d2	♖c2
38	♕xb4	♗xb4

Black still has threats, but they can be refuted if White keeps his head.

39	♖d8	f6
40	♖f1	fxe5
41	♖xe8+	♔g7
42	♘b3	♗c3+
43	♔b1	♖b2+
44	♔c1	♖xb3
45	♔c2	

Forking Black's last remaining pieces.

Black resigns

Having eliminated Karpov in the semi-final, the match which finally qualified Nigel Short through to his challenge of 1993 against Kasparov was against the Dutch Grandmaster Jan Timman.

World Championship Candidates Final, El Escorial 1993

	1	2	3	4	5	6	7	8	9	10	11	12	13	
Short	½	0	1	1	½	½	0	½	1	1	0	1	½	7½
Timman	½	1	0	0	½	½	1	½	0	0	1	0	½	5½

Game 10 was the final demonstration of who was in charge. After this game Short always looked like a clear winner. A game that, in its simplicity of means, yet crushing effects, recalls the best days of Bobby Fischer.

**Short – Timman
Candidates Final, Game 10,
El Escorial 1993
Ruy Lopez**

1	e4	e5
2	♘f3	♘c6
3	♗b5	a6

4   &a4   &f6

Yet another Ruy Lopez opening. It was extraordinary just how popular this variation was in the Short – Timman match. Could it have been the presence of books by Ruy Lopez himself, the 16th century Spanish chess theoretician, in the library of the adjacent Escorial fortress which inspired this devotion amongst the players?

5	0-0	&e7
6	&e1	b5
7	&b3	d6
8	c3	0-0
9	h3	&b7
10	d4	&e8
11	&bd2	&f8
12	d5 *(72)*	

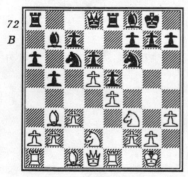

72
B

A little known choice, varying from the 12 a4 which has been habitually chosen by Kasparov and the rather feeble 12 &c2 with which Short lost quickly as White in game 2 of the same match. Nigel's move boldly gains space in the centre and drives the black queen's knight back to its stable.

12	...	&b8
13	&f1	&bd7
14	&g3	&c5
15	&c2	a5

This activity on the queen's wing seems irrelevant. If Black wanted to rupture the centre by means of ... c6, now was the time to do it. By vacillating he gives White the chance to improve his position.

| 16 | &h2 | g6 |
| 17 | &f3 | h5 *(73)* |

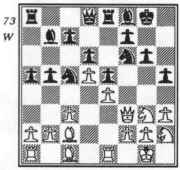

73
W

Timman's hyperactivity with his rook's pawns achieves only the goal of undermining his own position. Black's play is clearly that of one who has become demoralised.

18	&e3	&fd7
19	&ad1	&e7
20	&gf1	&g7
21	&c1	c6

Quite mistimed. This thrust, although playable six moves earlier, now permits White to drive the black knight to the edge of the board, saddle Black with a backward pawn on d6 and finally it encourages White to position his king's bishop on a superbly aggressive diagonal. Almost any other 21st move by Black would have been preferable.

22	b4	axb4
23	cxb4	♘a4
24	dxc6	♗xc6
25	♗b3	♖ad8
26	♕g3	

The threat is now ♕xg6 followed by a brutal demolition of Black's king's fortress. If Black seeks to parry this with 26 ... ♔h7 then 27 ♘f3 f6 28 ♘h4 ♘f8 29 ♕f3 with the terrible threat of ♘xg6.

26	...	♘f8
27	♘f3	♘e6
28	♘g5	♘xg5
29	♗xg5	♗f6
30	♗xf6	♕xf6
31	♖d3 *(74)*	

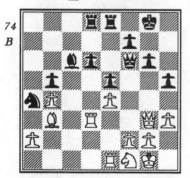

74
B

White's attack plays itself, his pieces feeding over harmoniously to establish decisive pressure against Black's wounds in the f-file.

31	...	h4
32	♖f3	

This is the key to White's victory. By ignoring the attack against his own queen, White breaks through to win a key pawn, whilst maintaining his pressure.

32	...	hxg3
33	♖xf6	gxf2+
34	♔xf2	♖e7
35	♖xg6+	♔h7
36	♖g3	d5
37	exd5	♗xd5
38	♖d3	♘b6
39	♘e3	♖ed7
40	♘xd5	

Black resigns

To my amazement some organs of the British chess press have been whingeing about Nigel Short's achievements in tournaments. Nobody can complain about his brilliant record in matches and to me it seems churlish to try to undermine the public record of Short's tournament successes. Admittedly, the 1993 world challenger has suffered some serious reverses in tournaments, such as Swift 1987 and Linares 1992. Nevertheless, as I shall proceed to demonstrate the British title aspirant has good reason to be proud of his tournament record in recent years.

Here are the final scores from Nigel's victories in two of the strongest Hastings tournaments and a complex game against his arch-rival Jon Speelman.

Hastings 1987/88
Short 9/14; Speelman 8½; Larsen 8; Psakhis, Chandler 7; Nunn, Benjamin 6½; Davies 3½.

Hastings 1988/89
Short 9/14; Korchnoi 8½; Speelman, Smyslov, Gulko 7½; Kosten, Larsen 6; Chandler 4.

Short – Speelman
Hastings 1987/88

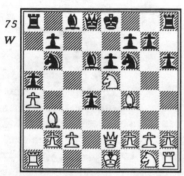

75
W

| 13 | 0-0-0 |

Short temporarily sacrifices a pawn in order to accentuate his lead in development.

13	...	0-0
14	♘gf3	♘bd5
15	♗g3	b5

Not to be outdone, Speelman hurls material back at his opponent in order to seize the initiative and bring the struggle closer to the white king.

16	♘c6	♕c7
17	axb5	a4
18	♗xd5	♘xd5
19	♘fxd4	a3
20	c4	a2
21	♔c2	e5
22	cxd5	exd4 *(76)*

Black's attack is reaching its

climax. White must now provide a haven for his king against the threat of ... ♗f5+.

76
W

23	b3	♗d7
24	♕c4	♗xc6
25	dxc6	♗xg3
26	hxg3	♕e5
27	c7	d3+
28	♔xd3	♕f5+
29	♔c3	♕xf2
30	♖hf1	♕e3+
31	♔b2	♖ac8
32	♖c1	♕e5+
33	♕c3	a1♕+

Black's passed pawn is doomed in any case, so it makes sense to sacrifice it now, so that White's king cannot use it as shelter.

34	♔xa1	♕xb5
35	♖f2	♖fe8
36	♖d2	♕b6
37	♔b2	♖e7

38	♖d8+	♖xd8
39	cxd8♕+	♕xd8
40	♕c8	♖e2+
41	♔a3	♕xc8
42	♖xc8+	♔h7
43	♖c3	♖xg2
44	b4	♖e2
45	b5	♔g6
46	b6	♖e6?? *(77)*

77
W

This wild and wonderful game should have ended in a draw if Black had instead played the immediate 46 ... ♖e8. In that case, White would doubtless, by advancing his king, promote his b-pawn to a queen and therefore win Black's rook. Black, on the other hand could push forwards his three to one pawn majority on the other flank and force White eventually to give his rook up for a black passed pawn. Such drawn endings can look complicated but are quite standard in grandmaster play. Instead, hypnotised by the various complications, Speelman hallucinates.

47 b7

Black resigns

If 47 ... ♖e8 48 ♖c8, while 47 ... ♖a6+ 48 ♔b2 ♖b6+ 49 ♖b3! (the move Black had overlooked) terminates Black's resistance. The tension of this needle game had been too much for Speelman. Had he drawn, he, rather than Short could have won the tournament.

Nigel has an uncanny knack of winning the decisive game in the last round. In this respect he recalls Emanuel Lasker, always at his most deadly with his back up against the wall and just one game to go. Nigel's latest exploit in this vein, before his challenge to Kasparov in 1993, was his last minute win against Vishy Anand, from the Euwe Memorial Tournament in Amsterdam.

This win against Anand by Nigel was of paramount psychological importance, given the extraordinarily high regard in which the champion, Garry Kasparov, seems to hold the Indian Grandmaster. Referring to their world title bout in London, Malcolm Pein's magazine *Chess Monthly* published an interview with Garry Kasparov, which included the following assessment, in response to the question, "Does Short have a chance to beat you?" - Kasparov replied - "Honestly speaking, no. I stated earlier that my challenger will be Short and that the match will be short. In fact I believe that there will be no fight about the title. I will surely win, but I consider it my duty as World Champion to win convincingly and show the world some exciting chess. That is my obligation and I am fully aware of it." In response to the question "Is Short the most dangerous opponent for you?" Kasparov replied: "No, I don't think so. Anand would have been a more dangerous player to deal with. He surely would have been the most difficult opponent at the present time."

The outcome of Nigel's final game against Anand therefore assumed huge importance.

Short – Anand
Amsterdam 1993
Petroff Defence

1	e4	e5
2	♘f3	♘f6

The Petroff is often construed as an attempt to reach an easy draw. In this case, a draw would certainly have suited Anand, since it would have given him undivided first prize in the tournament.

3	♘xe5	d6
4	♘f3	♘xe4
5	d4	d5
6	♗d3	♘c6
7	0-0	♗e7
8	c4	♘b4
9	♗e2	♗e6
10	♘c3	0-0

11	♗e3	♗f5
12	♘e5	(78)

This is a theoretical novelty which leads to sharp play. The most common previous move was 12 ♖c1, as used previously by Short against Timman at Hilversum in 1989.

12	...	♗f6
13	g4	♗e6
14	f4	♘xc3
15	bxc3	♘c6
16	♗f3	♗xe5
17	dxe5	d4
18	cxd4	♗xc4 (79)

White's next move is both compulsory and compelling. If White seeks to avoid the loss of the exchange by moving his king's rook Black will establish a light-square blockade in the centre of the board by means of ... ♘d5.

19	d5	♘e7
20	♗c5	♗xf1
21	♔xf1	♕d7
22	♕b3	

White has enormous compensation for the loss of the exchange in terms of the two bishops and a highly mobile pawn front.

| 22 | ... | b6 |

After the game Anand pinpointed this as his error, preferring the variation 22 ... c6 23 d6 ♘g6, which he considered perfectly playable.

| 23 | ♗a3 | ♖ae8 |
| 24 | ♖d1 | ♘g6 (80) |

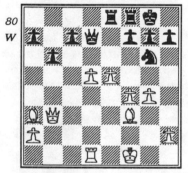

Black seeks salvation by returning the exchange and transposing to an endgame.

25	e6	♕d8
26	f5	♘e5
27	♗e2	♕h4
28	♕g3	♕xg3
29	hxg3	fxe6
30	♗xf8	♔xf8
31	dxe6	♔e7
32	g5	c6

33	g4	g6
34	♖d4	gxf5
35	gxf5	♖f8
36	♖f4	b5
37	♔e1 (81)	

| 37 | ... | h6 |

According to Anand and Pein 37 ... ♔d6 loses to 38 ♖d4+ ♔c5 39 e7 ♖e8 40 f6 ♔xd4 41 ♗h5 ♘g6 42 ♗xg6 hxg6 43 ♔ moves followed by f7 when a pawn queens. Still, even in this line, 38 ... ♔e7! should defend.

38	gxh6	♖h8
39	♖e4	♔f6
40	e7	♔xf5
41	♖xe5+	

Black resigns

♗h5 is coming and it will win a piece.

Nigel's one victory in the World Championship match:

**Short – Kasparov
Times World Championship,
Game 16, London 1993**

In this position Short had the choice to play wildly, as so often before in the match, or safely. He chose the latter.

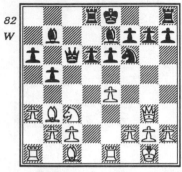

14 f3

14 ♘d5 is a thematic sacrifice, but after 14 ... exd5 15 exd5
♘xd5 16 ♕xg7 ♔d7 17 ♕g4+ (17
♕xf7 ♖de8 18 ♗g5 ♖hg8 19
♗xe7 ♖xg2+ 20 ♔xg2 ♘e3+ 21
♔g3 ♕g2+ 22 ♔f4 ♕e4+ 23 ♔g5
h6+ 24 ♔h5 ♕g4+ 25 ♔xh6
♖h8+ 26 ♕h7 ♘f5 checkmate) 17
... ♔c7 18 ♗xd5 ♕xd5 19 ♖xe7+
♔b8, the complications favour
Black, who has a massive
threat of ... ♖hg8.

14	...	0–0
15	♗h6	♘e8
16	♔h1	♔h8
17	♗g5	♗xg5
18	♕xg5	♘f6
19	♖ad1	♖d7
20	♖d3	♖fd8
21	♖ed1	♕c5
22	♕e3	♔g8
23	♔g1	♔f8
24	♕f2	♗a8 *(83)*

The purpose behind this
move has eluded most com-
mentators. However, the reason is quite clear once one
grasps the intention behind
Kasparov's 25th move. The

world champion's concept was
to entice the white knight onto
the d4 square, then prod it with
... e5 and in response to ♖c3 he
wanted to be able to retreat his
queen to a defended square.
The point of 24 ... ♗a8 is to
allow the black rook on d7 to
defend a7, the intended haven
for the black queen.

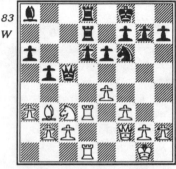

25 ♘e2 g6

Clearly designed to stop
White's knight going to f5 after
... e5. Nevertheless, Kasparov
should have exchanged queens.

26 ♘d4 *(84)*

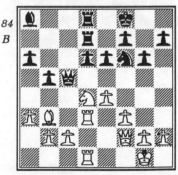

This is where Kasparov had
originally wanted to play 26 ...
e5, but now observed that his
variation did not work. Thus 26

... e5 27 ♖c3 ♕a7 (the defended square, but not 27 ... ♕b6 on account of 28 ♘e6+ picking up Black's queen) 28 ♘c6 ♕xf2+ 29 ♔xf2 ♖c8 (if 29 ... ♗xc6 30 ♖xc6 leaves Black with a terrible endgame) but now the devilish trick 30 ♘xe5 ♖xc3 31 ♘xd7+ winning. Or 30 ♘xe5 dxe5 31 ♖xc8+ when Black's position totally collapses.

26	...	♕e5
27	♖e1	g5
28	c3	♔g7
29	♗c2	♖g8
30	♘b3	♔f8
31	♖d4	♔e7
32	a4	h5
33	axb5	axb5
34	♖b4	h4
35	♘d4	g4

Short's next move is the fastest way to wrap things up. Much less convincing is 36 ♘f5+ exf5 37 exf5 gxf3 38 ♖xe5+ dxe5 when Black might struggle on.

36	♖xb5	d5
37	♕xh4	♕h5

38 ♘f5+ (85)

85
B

Black resigns

After 38 ... exf5 39 exf5+ ♔f8 40 ♕xf6 ♗b7 41 ♖xb7 ♖xb7 42 ♕d8+ ♔g7 43 f6+ ♔h8 44 ♕xg8+ ♔xg8 45 ♖e8 is checkmate, as pointed out by Dominic Lawson.

Finally a direct hit, after so many excellent positions had slipped out of Nigel's grasp. When Kasparov resigned game 16, the audience at the Savoy Theatre erupted in wild cheering and applause. Short's comment was: "Not before time".

5   Viswanathan Anand

Player's Name: Viswanathan Anand
Date of Birth: 11 December 1969
Nationality: Indian
Main Strengths
Tactical genius. Often terrifies opponents with his sight of the board in complex situations and his hyper-fast speed of moving.
Main Weaknesses
Impulsive and prone to blunder. Sometimes moves too quickly and without due thought.

It is one of the mysteries of chess that India, the most likely birthplace of the game, has produced so few masters of the art. In the 19th century there was the Brahmin Moheshunder Bonnerjee, who contested some interesting games with Cochrane in Calcutta. But it is not until the advent of Sultan Khan in the late 1920s that one can speak in terms of a true Indian grandmaster. Sultan Khan arrived in London as part of the retinue of an Indian nobleman Sir Umar Hayat Khan, ADC to King George V. Master and servant were, in spite of the identity of their last names, obviously not related.

While in London (which he detested because of the weath-er) Sultan Khan annihilated the best British masters, won the British Championship and ended up being promoted to top board of the British Empire team in the chess olympics. During the course of this triumphal career he inflicted defeat on Capablanca, Flohr, Tartakower and other recognized grandmasters. But after six years at the top Sir Umar whisked him back to India and Sultan Khan never again played a top class chess game. The whole Sultan Khan episode is simultaneously glorious and tragic. Had he stayed at his post Sultan Khan might have become world champion. For decades India languished with no prospect of another champion, but all this has recently changed with the comet-like progress of Viswanathan Anand.

Anand legitimately could become world champion. He has won one of the strongest recorded tournaments in the history of chess, the category 18 event at Reggio Emilia in Italy and he is the only grandmaster who has regularly inflicted defeat on both Karpov and Kasparov. Although he was eliminated from the 1990/93 world championship cycle by the narrowest of margins, by Karpov, the match was extremely close and on the general run of play, Anand missing many easy wins in several games, one might have expected Anand to go through rather than the former world champion.

Anand will be a major force in the next championship cycle and, along with Short, he could be considered one of the three most likely challengers for 1995. In particular he is feared for the demon speed of his play, often taking minutes, where others would take hours, to decide over his moves. In his home country, particularly in Calcutta where he has shared first prize in the Goodricke International Tournament, he is feted as a national hero. Teenage groupies clamour for his autograph, he is mobbed in the streets, restaurants open specially for him and when he arrived at the tournament he was showered with petals, a red carpet was quite literally rolled out and the tournament organizers presented him with a car.

It was at Tilburg 1991 that Anand made a real breakthrough. He became only the second player ever to beat both Karpov and Kasparov in the same event (Ivanchuk being the first at Linares earlier the same year). Little over a year previously I would have classed Anand as no more than a promising grandmaster, now he must be regarded as a definite future candidate for the world title itself.

Anand – Kasparov
Tilburg 1991/92
Sicilian Defence

1	e4	c5
2	♘f3	d6
3	d4	cxd4
4	♘xd4	♘f6
5	♘c3	a6
6	f4	e6
7	♕d3	♘bd7
8	0–0	

8 ♘f3 is considered normal. The text offers an unclear pawn sacrifice.

8	...	♕b6
9	♕e3	♕xb2
10	♘db5	*(86)*

After this piece sacrifice

both Black's king and his queen are in danger.

86 B			

10	...	axb5
11	♘xb5	♖a5
12	♖b1	♖xb5
13	♖xb2	♖xb2
14	♕a1	

Trapping Black's rook but Kasparov still retains substantial material compensation for his lost queen.

14	...	♖b6
15	♗xb6	♘xb6
16	♕c3	♗e7
17	♖b1	♘fd7
18	♕xg7	♗f6
19	♕h6	♔e7
20	♗b5	♖g8

After the game Kasparov claimed that 20 ... e5 would have given him the upper hand.

21	♖d1	e5
22	f5	♘c5
23	♖xd6 *(87)*	

87 B			

This sacrifice is murderous in that 23 ... ♔xd6 24 ♕xf6+ leads to carnage.

23	...	♗g5
24	♕xh7	♘xe4
25	♖xb6	♖d8
26	♗d3	♗e3+
27	♔f1	♗xb6
28	♗xe4	♖d4
29	c3	

A rapier-like final touch. After 29 ... ♖xe4 30 f6+ wins Black's rook. Therefore **Black resigned**.

Reggio Emilia 1991/92
Anand 6/9; Kasparov, Gelfand 5½; Karpov 5; Ivanchuk, Khalifman, Polugaevsky 4½; Salov, M Gurevich 4; Beliavsky 1½.

Kasparov – Anand
Reggio Emilia 1991
French Defence

1	e4	e6
2	d4	d5
3	♘d2	c5
4	exd5	♕xd5
5	dxc5	

A curious decision which should not present Black with severe problems since it assists his development. More testing is 5 ♘gf3 cxd4 6 ♗c4 ♕d6 7

0-0 ♘f6 as in Adams - Speelman, Duncan Lawrie English
Championship, London 1991.

5	...	♗xc5
6	♘gf3	♘f6
7	♗d3	0-0
8	♕e2	♘bd7
9	♘e4	b6

Black does not need to fear
the loss of the bishop pair
since he obtains sufficient
compensation in the speedy
mobilization of his forces.

| 10 | ♘xc5 | ♕xc5 |

If 10 ... ♘xc5, 11 ♗c4 would
go some way towards justifying
White's choice of variation.

11	♗e3	♕c7
12	♗d4	♗b7
13	0-0-0	♘c5 *(88)*

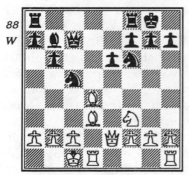

The world champion, even
after his somewhat lacklustre
opening, has still created a
situation which is full of tension. The players have castled
on opposite wings, which normally betokens a fierce
struggle and White's bishops
are aimed menacingly at the
black king. It should be noted,
though, that if White tries to

strike immediately and break
up Black's kingside pawns with
14 ♗xf6 then the *zwischenzug*
14 ... ♕f4+ intending to meet 15
♔b1 with 15 ... ♕xf6 guarantees
Black a perfectly acceptable
position.

| 14 | ♗e5 | ♘xd3+ |

Hastening to eliminate one
of White's most dangerous
attacking units.

| 15 | ♖xd3 | ♕c4 |

The black queen switches
into counter-attacking mode.
White's best now is probably 16
b3 ♕e4 followed by the exchange of queens with a likely
draw. Instead of pursuing this
arid course, Kasparov boldly
launches into an obscure attacking scheme, but in the
course of this he is tactically
outmanoeuvred by the young
Indian.

| 16 | ♘d4 | ♗e4 |
| 17 | ♖e3 | ♕xa2 |

If now 18 ♖xe4 ♕a1+ 19 ♔d2
♘xe4+ 20 ♕xe4 ♕xh1 21 ♕g4
Black's safest to beat off the
attack is 21 ... f6 22 ♘xe6 ♖fd8+
winning. Kasparov's choice on
move 18 appears decisive but
there is a remarkable resource
in the offing.

| 18 | ♗xf6 | ♗g6! |

Of course Black cannot
recapture on f6 since his bishop
is hanging but now White must
cope with the dual threats of ...
gxf6 and ... ♕a1+, so his hand is
forced.

| 19 | ♖a3 | ♕d5 *(89)* |

Kasparov is a piece ahead but he cannot retain his extra material. Furthermore his king has become weakened by the disappearance of his a2-pawn. If now 20 ♘e5 f6 and White cannot protect both his minor pieces. White's best then is 21 ♘d6 ♕xd6 (not 21 ... ♖fe8 22 ♘b5) 22 ♕xe6+ ♕xe6 23 ♘xe6 ♖fc8 24 ♘d4 ♖c4 when 25 ♖d1 leads to a very drawish position. In trying for more than this Kasparov runs enormous risks.

20	h4?	gxf6
21	h5	♕xd4
22	hxg6	hxg6
23	♖ah3	

White is now two pawns down but was doubtless relying on his attack in the h-file to generate adequate compensation.

| 23 | ... | f5 |

If here 24 ♖h8+ ♕xh8 25 ♖xh8+ ♔xh8 Black's two rooks and two pawns would triumph against White's queen in the endgame.

| 24 | ♖h4 | f4 |

25	♕f3	♖ac8
26	♖xf4	♕c5
27	c3	♔g7 (90)

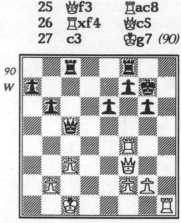

28 ♖hh4

This move is incomprehensible and after it White stays a pawn down with an exposed king so the outcome can no longer be in doubt. It looks more natural to play 28 ♖fh4 though after 28 ... ♕g5+ 29 ♔b1 ♕f5+ 30 ♕xf5 gxf5 White would still have to struggle to draw the endgame a pawn down. This would however have been better than what occurred in the game.

28	...	♕e5
29	g3	♕e1+
30	♔c2	♖cd8
31	♖d4	♕e5
32	♖hf4	♕c7
33	♕e3	e5
34	♖xd8	♖xd8
35	♖e4	♖d5
36	g4	b5
37	g5	♕d6
38	f3	a5 (91)

The beginning of the end. The advance of Black's pawns soon strips away the defences around White's king.

91 W		
39	♕e2	♛e6
40	♕h2	♛f5
41	♕g3	♛d7
42	♕e1	b4
43	cxb4	♛a4+
44	b3	♛a2+
45	♔c3	a4
46	bxa4	♛a3+
47	♔c2	♛xa4+
48	♔c3	♛a3+
49	♔c2	♖d3

White resigns

Anand – Kasparov
Paris Immopar 1992
Sicilian Defence

1	e4	c5
2	♘f3	d6
3	d4	cxd4
4	♘xd4	♘f6
5	♘c3	a6
6	f4	e6
7	♕f3	♛b6
8	a3	♘bd7

Of course not 8 ... ♛xd4? 9 ♗e3 trapping the queen.

9	♘b3	♛c7
10	g4	h6
11	h4	h5

12	g5	♘g4
13	♕d2	b5
14	♗h3	♘b6
15	0-0-0	♘c4
16	♗xg4	hxg4
17	♕xg4	*(92)*

This variation has become popular in grandmaster circles of late and has been especially practised by the younger Russians, such as Smirin. Black offers a pawn as a decoy on the kingside in order to prosecute his offensive against the white king. However, the most recent examples tend to prove that White's material advantage is of greater weight than Black's temporary initiative.

17	...	♖b8
18	g6	a5
19	♘d4	b4
20	♘cb5	♛c5
21	a4	e5
22	♘f5	f6
23	♕e2	♗xf5
24	exf5	*(93)*

Kasparov now decides to sacrifice rook for knight in order to mobilize his queenside pawns. A sure sign, though, that all is not well with his position is that he has still not energized his kingside forces.

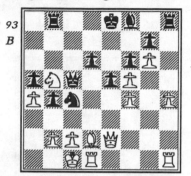

93
B

24	...	♖xb5
25	axb5	a4
26	♔b1	♕xb5
27	♕d3	b3
28	♔a1	♗e7
29	♗c1	♔d7
30	♖h2	

A fine and deep defensive move, the full significance of which only becomes apparent five moves later.

30	...	♖c8
31	h5	e4
32	♕d5	♖c5
33	♕e6+	♔d8
34	c3	a3
35	bxa3	(94)

94
B

This move beats off Black's attack but it is only possible because of the cunning placement of White's laterally-defending rook on h2.

35	...	♕a4
36	♖d4	♕a6
37	♖xe4	♖c7
38	♕g8+	

The decisive penetration.

| 38 | ... | ♔d7 |
| 39 | ♖he2 | |

Black resigns

After this temporary setback Kasparov won the next two games to clinch the final three to one in his favour.

A match which would have attracted great attention, had it not been for the Fischer – Spassky circus in Belgrade at the same time, was the clash between two of the foremost young pretenders to Kasparov's throne. Anand challenged the great white hope from the Ukraine, Vassily Ivanchuk. It is suspected that Ivanchuk is probably the most talented player in the world (apart from Kasparov himself) and, indeed, he has on occasion advanced to slot number two on the world ranking list, ahead of Karpov. It is also universally recognized that Ivanchuk's chief weakness is an excessively nervous disposition, which has led him into all sorts of personal setbacks and eccentricities during chess competitions.

In some tournaments Ivanchuk has been known to bang gongs during the rounds, or run into the street and start to screech at passers-by, while at Linares 1990 he had to be given a sedative before his last round game against Gelfand before it was even possible to bring him to the board. In the match against Anand this failure of nerve came prominently to the fore and instead of achieving the victory which the statistics had predicted, Ivanchuk suffered a humiliating defeat.

Linares Match 1992

	1	2	3	4	5	6	7	8	
Anand	1	1	½	½	½	½	0	1	5
Ivanchuk	0	0	½	½	½	½	1	0	3

The prize for the winner was $2000 and a new car, which seems faintly ridiculous when compared with the millions on offer for veterans Fischer and Spassky in Belgrade.

Anand – Ivanchuk
Linares Match, Game 8, 1992

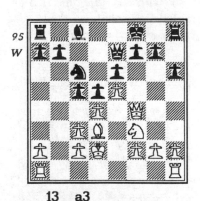

95
W

13 a3

White wants to stop ... cxd4 followed by ... ♛a3.

13	...	♗d7
14	♖hb1	b6

15	♕e3	♘a5
16	♔e1	♖c8
17	♔f1	♔e8
18	♔g1	♔d8
19	h3	♔c7

Black could draw easily with the blockading move ... c4. However, in order to tie the match Ivanchuk had to win, hence this risky procedure.

20	♗a6	♖b8
21	dxc5	*(96)*

96
B

21	...	♕xc5

This gives away the d4-square, after which White makes all the running. If he

wanted to play for a win he had
to risk 21 ... bxc5 and follow up
with ... ♖b6.

22	♘d4	♘c4
23	♕f4	♖hf8
24	♖b4	b5
25	♖ab1	♖b6

Trying to trap White's bishop, but Black is always a tempo
too late. If instead 25 ... ♘xa3
26 ♖1b3 ♘c4 27 ♘xb5+ ♗xb5 28
♖xb5 ♖xb5 29 ♖xb5 with a
great advantage to White.

26	♘xb5+	♗xb5
27	♖xb5	♕xa3
28	♖xb6	♘xb6
29	♕d4	*(97)*

| 29 | ... | ♖b8 |

Of course 29 ... ♕xa6 fails to
30 ♕c5+.

30	♗b5	♖b7
31	♖b3	♕e7
32	♗a6	♖b8
33	c4	dxc4
34	♗xc4	♖d8
35	♕e4	♔b8
36	♗e2	♕c7
37	♗f3	

Black lost on time

It is a measure of Ivanchuk's
demoralization in this match
that he should here have lost
on time. Of course, Black's
position is extremely difficult
but it does not take a genius to
see that Black must quickly
play 37 ... ♔c8 when 38 ♖c3
(planning 38 ... ♕xc3 39 ♕b7
mate) fails to 38 ... ♖d1+! 39
♗xd1 ♕xc3 when Black is well
past the worst. All in all a
depressing experience for Ivanchuk who has still failed to establish himself as a convincing
claimant to the world crown.

Moscow 1992
Anand, Gelfand 4½/7; Kamsky 4; Yusupov, Salov, Karpov 3½;
Shirov 3; Timman 1½.

Anand – Timman
Moscow 1992

A standard position from the
Semi-Tarrasch variation of the
Queen's Gambit Declined, into
which this opening has trans-
posed, from an initial Caro-
Kann. White has attacking

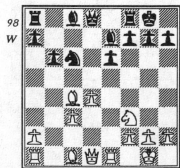

prospects against Black's king, but Black has a solid and resilient position, with possibilities of long-term play against White's hanging pawns on c3 and d4.

12	♗d3	♗b7
13	h4	

Even this pawn sacrifice is known. Should Black accept with 13 ... ♗xh4, then 14 ♘xh4 ♕xh4 15 ♖e3 conjures up all sorts of unpleasant threats against Black's kingside.

13	...	♕d5
14	♖b1	♖ac8
15	♖b5	♕d6
16	d5 *(99)*	

99
B

An extraordinary move which is, in fact inferior, to the more thematic 16 ♘g5. Nevertheless, this unexpected move seems to exert an unsettling effect on Timman, who promptly proceeds to commit an appalling blunder.

16	...	♗a6??

A total aberration which simply loses substantial material for no tangible compensation. Black would have been safe after 16 ... ♘d8. Timman must have been mesmerized by the erroneous thought that his only alternative to the text was 16 ... exd5 17 ♖xd5 ♕xd5 which would of course have been fatal after 18 ♗xh7+ ♔xh7 19 ♕xd5.

17	dxc6	♖fd8
18	♕a4	

If Timman had expected to regain his material investment, this shot is a rude awakening. After 18 ... ♗xb5 19 ♗xb5 Black's case is hopeless but what he plays is no better.

18	...	♕xd3
19	♕xa6	♖xc6
20	♗e3	♗f6
21	♗d4	♗xd4
22	cxd4	♖c3
23	a4	♖a3
24	♕xa7	♕xb5
25	♕e7	Black resigns

Anand – Timman
Linares 1993
Ruy Lopez

1	e4	e5
2	♘f3	♘c6
3	♗b5	a6
4	♗a4	b5
5	♗b3	♘a5
6	0-0	d6
7	d4	♘xb3 *(100)*

Black gains the two bishops and doubles White's pawns with this rather unsubtle defence to the Ruy Lopez. However, if chess were that simple, the Ruy Lopez would have gone out of fashion in the 16th century already.

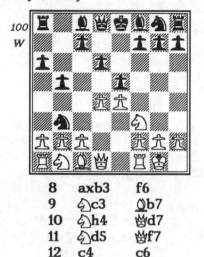

8	axb3	f6
9	♘c3	♗b7
10	♘h4	♕d7
11	♘d5	♕f7
12	c4	c6
13	♘e3	♘e7
14	d5	

This establishes White's dominance in the centre and on the queenside.

14	...	cxd5
15	cxd5	g6
16	♗d2	f5 (101)

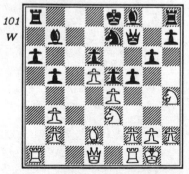

Has Timman never heard of development? It is usually fatal to launch an attack when your opponent has strategic advan-

tages, is better coordinated and has far more of his pieces in play.

17	♖c1	♖c8
18	♖xc8+	♗xc8
19	exf5	gxf5
20	♘b4	f4 (102)

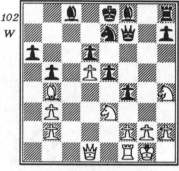

21 ♗xd6!

It is hardly surprising, with Black's army slumbering in their beds, that White can finish things off with a sacrificial flourish.

21	...	fxe3
22	fxe3	♕g7
23	♕c2	♗d7
24	♕c7	♕g5
25	♘f3	♕xe3+
26	♔h1	♗g7
27	♖e1	♕f4
28	♗xe7	♔xe7
29	♘xe5	**Black resigned**

He has been totally routed.

**Anand – Yusupov
FIDE Candidates Match,
Wijk aan Zee 1994
Ruy Lopez**

| 1 | e4 | e5 |

2	♘f3	♘c6
3	♗b5	a6
4	♗a4	d6
5	c3	f5 *(103)*

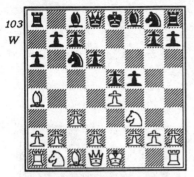

103
W

The Siesta Variation, so-called since it was widely held that Capablanca had introduced it against Steiner at the Siesta tournament of Budapest 1928. In fact, it was an invention of the fertile brain of the American Grandmaster Frank Marshall who first produced it against Capablanca himself in their match of 1909.

6   exf5

6 d4 fxe4 7 ♘g5 exd4 8 ♘xe4 ♘f6 9 ♗g5 was Réti – Capablanca, Berlin 1928.

6	...	♗xf5
7	0-0	

7 d4 e4 8 ♕e2 ♗e7 9 ♘fd2 ♘f6 10 h3 was Capablanca – Marshall, Match 1909 and 7 d4 e4 8 ♗g5 ♗e7 9 ♘h4 ♗e6 was Steiner – Capablanca, Budapest 1928. In all cases, Black has a perfectly good game. White's choice here had earlier been neglected through fear of the hole which arises on the d3

square.

7	...	♗d3
8	♖e1	♗e7
9	♗c2	

White hastens to expel the intruder.

9	...	♗xc2
10	♕xc2	♘f6
11	d4	0-0 *(104)*

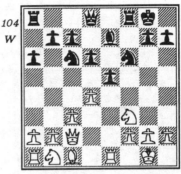

104
W

12   d5

For some time theory has believed that White can maintain a slight edge with 12 dxe5. The text is more ambitious.

12   ...   e4

Black pins his hopes on a counter-attack. The supine 12 ... ♘b8 leads to a great White advantage after 13 ♘g5 ♕c8 14 c4 as in the game Putzbach – Kreutzkamp played at Hamburg 1992. Of course 12 ... ♘xd5 fails to 13 ♕b3 winning the knight.

13	♘g5	♘e5
14	♘e6	♕d7

Yusupov hopes for 15 ♘xf8 when 15 ... ♕g4 would give him powerful threats. Anand prefers to maintain his muscular knight on e6, whilst targeting the black e-pawn.

15	♘d2	e3
16	♖xe3	♘xd5
17	♘xf8	♘xe3
18	♕xh7+	

This irruption essentially refutes Black's conception. Although Yusupov maintains material parity he suffers, in the further course of the game, from lack of adequate shelter for his king.

18	...	♔xf8 *(105)*

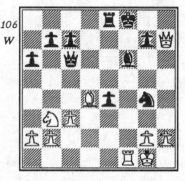

19   fxe3

The open f-file will be productive for the further prosecution of White's attack. White only has to avoid the greedy 19 ♕h8+ ♔f7 20 ♕xa8 when the tables are turned by 20 ... ♘xg2 and ... ♕g4 wreck-ing the protection around White's king.

19	...	♖e8
20	e4	d5
21	♘b3	dxe4
22	♗e3	♗f6
23	♖f1	

The threat is ♖xf6+ followed by ♗h6+.

23	...	♘g4
24	♗d4	♕c6 *(106)*

A blunder which loses a piece but even after the superior defence 24 ... ♕e6 25 ♘c5 maintains an overwhelming advantage.

25   ♗c5+
Black resigned

After 25 ... ♔f7 26 ♕h5+ his case is hopeless.

6 Michael Adams

Player's Name: Michael Adams
Date of Birth: 11 November 1971
Nationality: British
Main Strengths
Tactically and strategically sharp. Super rapid assimilation and understanding of changing events on the board.
Main Weaknesses
Defective knowledge of main line opening theory, particularly when defending as Black. Sometimes careless.

Michael Adams from Truro, who became the youngest ever British champion when he won the title in 1989 and was also the youngest British player ever to become a grandmaster, added a fresh triumph to his already illustrious career in the 1991 international tournament at Terrassa, a small town just outside Barcelona in Spain. Adams raced for the lead with the Estonian Grandmaster Jaan Ehlvest, and caught up with him when Ehlvest lost to his fellow countryman Epishin in the final round. Adams also beat Ehlvest in their individual encounter, which ensured him the victor's trophy on tie-break.

The game that will have given him most pleasure is the victory against Vassily Ivanchuk, who had smashed Kasparov's ten year record of winning every event in which he played, when Ivanchuk won the tournament at Linares, Spain in February earlier in the same year. Adams won a brilliant game against him, with the black pieces. Particularly spectacular was Adams' sacrifice of a rook on move 25 to strip away the protection from Ivanchuk's king. At the end of the game Ivanchuk's position was in ruins and he was faced with colossal loss of material. Adams played the entire game in daring gambit style. Even his opening, the Marshall Attack in the Ruy Lopez, demonstrated that Adams was neither offering nor asking for any quarter.

Michael Adams was characteristically modest about his achievement. In fact he did not let anybody know that he was even participating in such a strong tournament let alone that he had defeated the man who, in 1991 at least, was seen as the crown prince of the chess world. The first anybody in the UK spotted about the event was after we had been alerted by Nigel Short's Greek mother-in-law, when she noticed an item in an Athens newspaper. In stark contrast, the French prodigy Lautier had been singing his own praises quite vociferously, and the French magazine *Europe Echecs* quotes him as stating in an interview that he would have a 50% chance of victory in a match against Kasparov, while Kasparov would have a 50% chance of a draw. Such vainglorious croakings were put in sharp perspective by his result relative to our own star in Terrassa.

Terrassa 1991

Adams, Ehlvest 6½/9; Ivanchuk 5½; Romanishin, Epishin 5; Illescas 4½; Bonsch, Lautier 4; Garcia 2½; Pomes 1½.

Ivanchuk – Adams
Terrassa 1991
Ruy Lopez

1	e4	e5
2	♘f3	♘c6
3	♗b5	a6
4	♗a4	♘f6
5	0-0	♗e7
6	♖e1	b5
7	♗b3	0-0
8	c3	d5 *(107)*

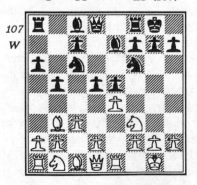

107 W

Frank Marshall's famous gambit, designed to seize the initiative at an early stage. It is also a favourite of Ivanchuk and therefore required some courage on Michael's part to employ it. Alternatively it was very cunning psychology.

9	exd5	♘xd5
10	♘xe5	♘xe5
11	♖xe5	c6
12	d4	♗d6
13	♖e1	♕h4
14	g3	♕h3
15	♗e3	

Timman – Ivanchuk from Linares 1991 diverged with 15 ♖e4 and ended in a highly unclear draw after 15 ... g5 16 ♕f3 ♗f5 17 ♗xd5 cxd5 18 ♖e3 ♗e4 19 ♖xe4 dxe4 20 ♕f6 ♕g4 21 ♘d2 ♖ae8 22 ♘f1 ♗e7 23

♛xa6 f5 24 ♛xb5 f4.

15	...	♗g4
16	♛d3	

To meet 16 ... ♗f3 with 17 ♛f1.

16	...	♖ae8
17	♘d2	♛h5

The latest try for Black. Older attempts which look plausible but are ultimately less successful are the immediate 17 ... ♖e6 and 17 ... f5.

18	♘f1	♖e6
19	♗d1	f5
20	♗xg4	♛xg4
21	♗d2	♖g6
22	♔g2	f4
23	f3	♛h5
24	g4	♛h4
25	♖e2?	*(108)*

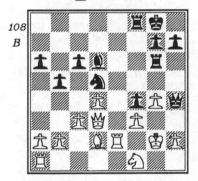

108
B

Walking directly into an ambush. His idea is clear, to prepare doubling rooks in the e-file by the manoeuvre ♗e1 - f2. This would have the effect of driving away the black queen and adding to the defences of the white king. However, Ivanchuk has overlooked an unpleasant shot. White would like to play 25 ♖e4 but this allows

... ♘f6 or 25 h3, but this allows ... ♖h6. Since White, in spite of his extra pawn, has no consolidating move available, it must be concluded that his position is already rather difficult.

| 25 | ... | ♖xg4+! |

This temporary sacrifice has the effect of exposing White's king and makes it virtually impossible for him to survive in the practical struggle.

26	fxg4	f3+
27	♔h1	fxe2
28	♛xe2	♔h8
29	♔g1	h6
30	♛g2	♗f4
31	♗e1	♛g5
32	h3	♛g6
33	♖d1	♗b8

It is very impressive over the last few moves how Adams has played such a controlled waiting game. He cannot break through with a direct attack but it soon becomes clear that White's position evinces targets both on the queenside as well as the kingside.

34	♖d2	♛b1
35	♗f2	♔g8 *(109)*

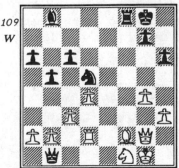

109
W

A very subtle move. White is so tied up that he is almost in zugzwang, i.e. any move that he makes will lead to a further deterioration of his position.

36 b3

Hoping for 36 ... ♘xc3 37 ♕xc6.

36	...	♗f4
37	♖e2	♘xc3
38	♖e6	♕xa2
39	♖xc6	♕xb3
40	♖xa6	♘e2+
41	♔h1	♗b8
42	♘e1	♕d1

White resigns

The only way to drag on his somewhat hopeless resistance would be by 43 ♖a1 ♕xa1 44 ♕xe2 but even in that case 44 ... ♖xf1+ 45 ♕xf1 ♗g3 nets a clear piece.

Garry Kasparov often jokes that he should be given honorary Scottish citizenship for his resurrection of the Scotch opening at world championship level. With the world champion setting the trend the grandmasters in the Foreign & Colonial Hastings tournament 1992 were only too willing to sample the delights of the Scotch.

Chandler – Adams
Foreign and Colonial
Hastings Premier
Scotch Game

1	e4	e5
2	♘f3	♘c6
3	d4	exd4
4	♘xd4	♘f6
5	♘xc6	bxc6
6	e5	♕e7
7	♕e2	♘d5
8	c4	♘b6

After 8 ... ♗a6 two Kasparov – Karpov encounters have seen 9 b3, e.g. 9 ... 0-0-0 (9 ... g6 10 f4 f6 11 ♗a3 ♕f7 12 ♕d2 ♘b6 13 c5 ♗xf1 14 cxb6 14... axb6 15 e6 dxe6 16 ♗xf8 Kasparov – Karpov, Tilburg Interpolis 1991) 10 g3 ♖e8 11 ♗b2 f6 12 ♗g2 fxe5 13 0-0 h5 14 ♕d2 Kasparov – Karpov, World Championship Game 14, Lyons 1990.

9	♘d2	♗b7
10	b3	0-0-0
11	♗b2	c5
12	0-0-0	d6

Black has chosen an interesting way of combatting White's opening. In exchange for weak pawns he gains free play for his bishops and major pieces. The Cinderella at Black's ball, though, is the knight on b6 which is very short of perspectives at the moment.

13 exd6 ♕xd6 *(110)*

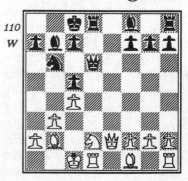

14 ♕g4+

This could be the start of a faulty plan. An interesting alternative is 14 g3 ♘xh1 15 ♘h3+ ♔b8 16 ♖xh1 ♕c6 17 ♖g1 with the plan of realigning White's king's bishop and queen along the vulnerable h1–a8 diagonal towards the black king. This idea may possibly form the basis for future theoretical investigation.

14 ... ♔b8
15 ♗e2 h5
16 ♕f5 ♕h6
17 ♘f3

After this, White's pieces get into a tangle. Chandler suggested as a possible improvement 17 f4 ♘d6 18 g3 ♘xh1 19 ♖xh1 but he rejected it because Black can force a trade of queens with either 19 ... ♕g6 or 19 ... ♕e6. After, for example, 19 ... ♕g6, though, with 20 ♕xg6 fxg6 21 ♘e4 White should have more than sufficient compensation to avoid losing.

17 ... ♗c8

An extremely strong move. The surrender of control to White's queen and bishop over the h1–a8 diagonal is purely deceptive since Black has complete command of the a8 and b7 squares. Meanwhile White's pieces are about to be driven from pillar to post.

18 ♕e4

This attack is illusory and temporary.

18 ... f5

19 ♕e3 g5!!

A brilliant idea. Not only do the black pawns continue to crowd White's pieces out of the game Black also offers a sacrifice which can hardly be accepted. After 20 ♘xh8 ♕xh8 White is exposed to withering fire in the long dark-squared diagonal.

20 ♕e5 ♗d6
21 ♕f6 g4
22 ♗e2

If White trades queens to try to break the pin against his knight on d2 Black still retains a huge advantage, for example 22 ♕xh6 ♖xh6 23 ♗e2 ♗f4 24 ♔c2 ♖hd6 25 ♗c3 ♗b7 with many threats.

22 ... ♕f4

Now Black's pieces pour in for the decisive attack.

23 f3 ♖he8
24 ♗d3 ♕e3
25 ♗c2 ♗f4
26 ♕c3 ♕f2

The threats are overwhelming: ... ♕xg2, ... ♖e2, ... ♗e5. White can think of nothing better than to surrender his queen for inadequate compensation.

27 g3 ♗e5
28 ♕xe5 ♖xe5
29 ♗xe5 gxf3
30 ♖hf1 ♕e2
31 ♗f4

If 31 ♘xf3 ♖xd1+ wins a piece.

31 ... f2
White resigns

Adams – Sadler
FIDE Zonal, Dublin 1993
Sicilian Defence

1	e4	c5
2	♘f3	d6
3	d4	cxd4
4	♘xd4	♘f6
5	♘c3	a6
6	♗c4	

This was a favourite of Bobby Fischer and has recently been adopted by both Short and Kasparov.

6	...	e6
7	♗b3	b5
8	0–0	♗b7
9	♖e1	♘bd7
10	♗g5	♕b6

This is an attempt to improve on the game Fischer – Rubinetti from the Palma de Mallorca Interzonal of 1970 which had gone 10 ... h6 11 ♗h4 ♘c5 12 ♗d5! exd5 13 exd5+ ♔d7 14 b4 ♘a4 15 ♘xa4 bxa4 16 c4 ♔c8 17 ♕xa4 with two pawns and a fierce attack for the sacrificed bishop.

11	a4	b4
12	♘d5 *(111)*	

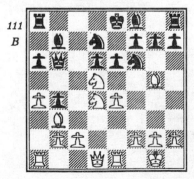

Exactly the same sacrificial attacking motif as in the Fischer game, but here White's onslaught is accelerated by the fact that it is most difficult for Black to retain his extra material. This is due to the inability of his king to flee from the perilous e-file, the primary avenue for White's aggression.

12	...	exd5
13	exd5+	♘e5
14	a5	♕c5
15	♗e3	♕c8
16	♗a4+	♔e7
17	f4	♘xd5
18	fxe5	dxe5
19	♕h5	f6
20	♗f2	g6
21	♖xe5+	

If 21 ... fxe5 22 ♕xe5+ wins the rook on h8.

21	...	♔f7
22	♕f3	♘c7
23	♕b3+	♔g7
24	♘f5+ *(112)*	

This final sacrifice demolishes the flimsy barricades defending the black king.

24	...	gxf5

25	♕g3+	♔f7
26	♗b3+	♘d5
27	♖xd5	

Black resigns

27 ... ♗xd5 28 ♗xd5+ ♔e8 29 ♖e1+ leads to a total massacre.

Kramnik – Adams
Biel FIDE Interzonal 1993

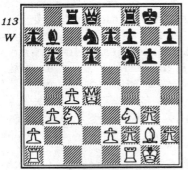

113
W

During the 1930s Capablanca and Botvinnik would regularly convert the type of space advantage White enjoys here into routine victories. Nowadays, it has been appreciated that Black's resilient hedgehog set-up is, in fact, an extraordinarily tough formation to pierce.

14	♖ac1	♖c5
15	b4	♖c8
16	a3	♖e8
17	e4	♕c7
18	♘d5	♕b8

Black must avoid making concessions, hence the queen retreat. To capture on d5 would alter the situation in White's favour.

19	♗h3	♖cd8

20	♘d2	♗a8
21	♗g2	a6
22	♘b3	♖c8
23	f4	♖cd8
24	♔h1	♘h5

This knight move sets a devilish trap.

| 25 | g4 | |

Kramnik falls straight into Black's snare. The cautious 25 ♕d2 would have been much superior.

| 25 | ... | ♘xf4!! (114) |

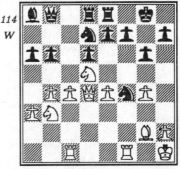

114
W

A frightful shock for White. The looming threat of ... e5 will regain the sacrificed material and leave White with a shattered position.

26	♘xf4	e5
27	♕f2	exf4
28	♕xf4	♘e5

The excellent position of this knight, blockading White's weak e4-pawn, virtually guarantees victory on its own.

29	♖c3	♕c7
30	♘d2	♕e7
31	g5	♖c8
32	♖fc1	b5
33	h4	♗b7
34	♔h2	♖c6 (115)

115
W

Anticipating the exchange of all the rooks, when the weaknesses around White's king's field will become acute.

	35	cxb5	axb5
	36	♘f1	♖ec8
	37	♖xc6	♖xc6
	38	♖xc6	♗xc6
	39	♘b3	♛a7

It has been apparent for some time that White's scattered forces would have no real defence to this penetration by the black queen.

	40	♘a5	♗d7
	41	♗e2	♛d4

Black's queen and knight dominate the board.

	42	♔g2	♛b2
	43	♛f2	♛xa3
	44	♛f6	♛h3+
	45	♔f2	♛xh4+
	46	♔e3	h5
	47	♘b7	♛e1

White resigns

Black threatens both ... ♗g4 and ... ♘g4+ and if 48 ♛xd6 then 48 ... ♘c4+ still wins the white queen. A sensational rout by Adams of a powerful opponent.

At the PCA world title qualifier, Groningen, December 1993, Anand was the pre-tournament favourite and having built up an early cache of wins, coasted home with draws. Michael Adams, on the other hand, lost one game towards the middle of the tournament and had to thunder home with a series of victories in order to ensure his qualification. Indeed, Adams was actually declared the official tournament winner on the basis of the tie-breaking system in force, namely the rating average of his opposition, which was 2645 as opposed to Anand's 2635.9. What impressed me most about Adams' performance was the Capablanca-like calm and method of his wins in the crucial games towards the end.

Adams – I. Sokolov
PCA Qualifier,
Groningen 1993
Ruy Lopez

1	e4	e5
2	♘f3	♘c6
3	♗b5	a6
4	♗a4	♘f6
5	0-0	♗e7
6	♖e1	b5
7	♗b3	0-0

Threatening to play the Marshall Attack, which Adams avoids.

8 d3

In his match against Short,

Kasparov regularly defused the Marshall with 8 a4 and this is an alternative method of achieving a similar aim.

8	...	d6
9	c3	♘a5
10	♗c2	c5
11	♘bd2	♘c6
12	♘f1	d5 *(116)*

116
W

It is always attractive to go for this kind of central break but the further course of this game shows why White tends to retain the initiative.

13	exd5	♛xd5
14	♗b3	♛d6
15	♛e2	♘d7
16	♘g3	♛c7
17	♘f5	♗d8
18	♘g5	♘f6
19	♛f3	♖b8
20	♘e4	♘xe4
21	dxe4	c4
22	♗c2	♘e7

This might appear to equalize but Adams has subtly perceived that he does not need to move his knight and can accept the liability of doubled pawns.

23	♛g3	♘xf5
24	exf5	♗f6

25 h4!

Cleverly increasing his command of terrain on the kingside.

25	...	♔h8
26	♗g5	♗b7
27	♖ad1	♖bd8
28	♛e3	*(117)*

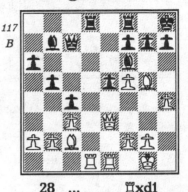

117
B

28	...	♖xd1

If Black's defence can be criticized it is here. The surrender of the d-file leads to severe problems for him. In particular, White's queen soon penetrates via a fresh avenue of attack into Black's camp.

29	♖xd1	♛e7
30	♛b6	♗c8
31	♗xf6	♛xf6
32	♛xf6	gxf6
33	♖d6	♔g7
34	♗e4	♖e8
35	g4	h6
36	♔h2	♖g8
37	♔g3	a5
38	a3	♖e8
39	f3	♖e7 *(118)*

This allows a tactical coup but Black had run out of moves. Moves like ... ♖h8 are clearly too passive and would allow White to pick off Black's queenside pawns with ♗c6.

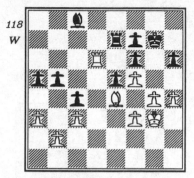

118
W

40 g5

Black cannot now capture twice on g5 due to f6+.

40	...	hxg5
41	hxg5	♖d7
42	gxf6+	♔h6
43	♖xd7	♗xd7
44	f4	exf4+
45	♔xf4	a4
46	♗d5	♗e8
47	♔g4	

This manoeuvre is essential to drive Black's king back before reverting to the decisive manoeuvre of ♔f4–e5 followed by mopping up Black's queenside pawns.

47	...	♔h7
48	♔g5	♔g8
49	♔f4	

Black resigns

Adams – Gulko
PCA Qualifier,
Groningen 1993

Gulko is an expert on the French, which had been the defence employed by Black in this game, but Adams has a formidable record on the White side, especially with the Tarrasch variation, including wins against Bronstein, Korchnoi, Short and Speelman.

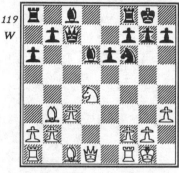

119
W

14	♖e1	b5
15	♗g5	♗b7
16	♗c2	♘d5
17	♕h5	g6

The position is almost equal but White enjoys a slightly freer game which might convert into a dangerous attack against even slightly inaccurate defence.

18	♕h4	♗h2+
19	♔h1	♗f4
20	♗e4	♖ab8

I do not like this move. Surely the rook would be more usefully employed on e8 or d8.

21	♖ad1	♗xg5
22	♕xg5	♘b6

Black should simplify with 22 ... ♕f4!.

23	♗xb7	♕xb7
24	♘f3	♘d5
25	♕h6	♖fd8
26	♖d4	

White's attacking plan crystallises, a crude but effective onslaught against the black pawn on h7.

26	...	♛e7
27	♖h4	♞f6
28	♞e5	

If 28 ♞g5, then 28 ... ♛f8 breaks the back of White's attack.

28	...	♖d6
29	♞g4	♖bd8
30	♞xf6+	♛xf6
31	♛xh7+	♚f8
32	♛h6+	♚g8
33	♖f4	♛g7
34	♛g5	♖d2
35	♛e7	♛f8
36	♖xe6	*(120)*

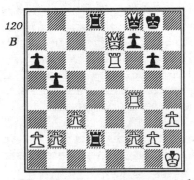

Transposing into an endgame where White's queen is more valuable than Black's rooks.

36	...	fxe6
37	♛xe6+	♚g7
38	♛e5+	♚g8
39	♖xf8+	♖xf8
40	♛g5	♖fxf2
41	♛xg6+	♚h8
42	♛h6+	♚g8
43	♛xa6	♖xb2 *(121)*

An admission of defeat.

Black cannot capture on g2 on account of ♛a8+ which would transpose into a won king and pawn endgame. Once this has become clear Black's resignation can only be postponed.

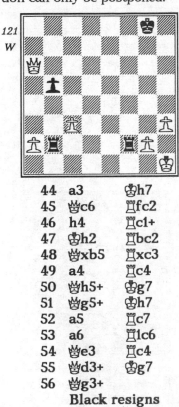

44	a3	♚h7
45	♛c6	♖fc2
46	h4	♖c1+
47	♚h2	♖bc2
48	♛xb5	♖xc3
49	a4	♖c4
50	♛h5+	♚g7
51	♛g5+	♚h7
52	a5	♖c7
53	a6	♖1c6
54	♛e3	♖c4
55	♛d3+	♚g7
56	♛g3+	

Black resigns

And now for Adams' masterpiece from the tournament.

**Kir. Georgiev – Adams
PCA Qualifier,
Groningen 1993
Caro–Kann Defence**

1	e4	c6
2	d4	d5

3	♘c3	dxe4
4	♘xe4	♘d7
5	♗c4	♘gf6
6	♘g5	

Accepting the challenge. I often played this variation for Black in tournaments and found that my opponents had a depressing tendency to simplify with 6 ♘xf6+ ♘xf6 7 ♘f3, with a position tending towards sterile equality.

6	...	e6
7	♕e2	

The threat is ♘xf7 with a quick checkmate to follow.

7	...	♘b6 *(122)*

122 W

8	♗d3

The main alternative is 8 ♗b3 but Karpov has been proving that Black's position is perfectly playable here as, for example, in Ivanchuk – Karpov, Tilburg 1993: 8 ... h6 9 ♘5f3 a5 10 a3 a4 11 ♗a2 c5 with reasonable counterplay.

8	...	h6

Evidently Black cannot capture on d4. If 8 ... ♕xd4 9 ♘1f3 followed by ♘e5 grants White an overwhelming lead in development.

9	♘5f3	c5
10	dxc5	♗xc5
11	♕d2	

It would seem more aggressive to play 11 ♘e5 which has, in fact, been the main line. However, the indefatigable Karpov has once again been responsible for drawing the teeth of this variation, e.g. 11 ... ♘bd7 12 ♘gf3 ♕c7 13 0-0 0-0 14 ♖e1 led to a draw in Ivanchuk – Karpov, Reykjavik World Cup 1991.

11	...	0-0
12	0-0-0	♘a4!

A theoretical novelty of tremendous depth and brilliance. Its invention has been variously credited to Julian Hodgson, William Watson and Jon Tisdall. The reason it had previously been overlooked was not just the decentralization of the knight but also the fact that White can now play to win a piece. Nevertheless, this concept is a prelude to a gradual attack against White's king.

13	♗b5

Resolutely heading down the main line. There are various ways to lose immediately, including 13 ♘e5 ♗d4 14 c3 ♗xe5, while 13 b3 ♗a3+ 14 ♔b1 ♘c5 is also unfavourable for White.

13	...	♗d7 *(123)*

Georgiev must originally have intended 14 ♗xa4 ♗xa4 15 ♕c4 but then a sample variation is 15 ... b5 16 ♕xc5 ♖c8 17

♕a3 ♗xc2 18 ♖e1 ♘e4 19 ♕e3 ♘xd2 20 ♕xd2 ♗f5+ 21 ♔d1 when 21 ... ♖c2 gives Black a winning attack.

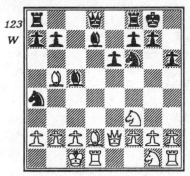

14 ♗xd7 ♕xd7
15 ♘h3

Changing horses in midstream like this is nearly always fatal. White had clearly intended to annex a pawn with 15 ♗xh6, discovering an attack from his rook against the black queen. But then he drew back after observing the complications of 15 ... ♘c3 16 bxc3 ♗a3+ 17 ♔b1 ♕c6 18 ♗c1 ♘e4 when he has to play 19 ♕xe4 ♕xe4 20 ♗xa3. Alternatively, Georgiev might have been frightened of 15 ... ♕c7 16 ♗e3 ♕b6 17 c3 ♗xe3+ 18 fxe3 ♖ac8 when White's pawns are weak and Black is concentrating force against the white king.

15 ... ♖ac8
16 ♔b1

As before, snatching a red-hot pawn with 16 ♗xh6 entails enormous risk, e.g. 16 ... ♕c6 17 ♗e3 ♕b6 emphasizing White's vulnerability on the b2-square,

for after 18 c3 ♗xe3+ 19 fxe3 ♘xc3 is terminal.

16 ... ♕c6
17 ♗c1 *(124)*

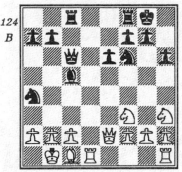

Accompanied by a draw offer which Adams naturally declined.

17 ... ♘d5
18 ♕c4 ♖fd8

After the game Adams claimed that 18 ... b5 at once would have been even more dangerous for White.

19 ♔a1

This is too passive. He should try 19 ♘e5. However, White must avoid 19 ♕g4 when 19 ... ♘dc3+ forces a quick win.

19 ... b5
20 ♕e4 ♗e7

Regrouping the bishop with tempo onto a more aggressive diagonal.

21 c3

The c2-pawn was under attack but now it represents a target for future black sacrifices.

21 ... ♕a6

Placing the black queen directly opposite White's king

announces obviously evil intentions.

22 ♘e5   ♗f6
23 ♘g4   ♘axc3

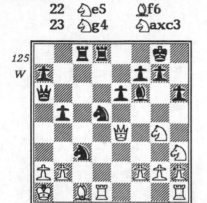

125
W

With so many pieces facing White's king it is hardly surprising that Black can crash through with a sacrificial combination. If 24 ♘xf6+ Black's reply 24 ... ♘xf6 leaves White's king and queen under threat.

24 bxc3   ♗xc3+
25 ♗b2   ♖c4
26 ♕f3   ♗xb2+
27 ♔xb2   ♖c2+

Sacrifices on empty squares are always attractive. This investment of a rook smokes White's king out into the open.

28 ♔xc2 (126)

Black's next move is absolutely natural and leads to a quick win. However, there is a faster checkmate, which could have been achieved in five

moves by the rather less natural-looking check 28 ... ♘b4+, for example, 29 ♔c1 (29 ♔c3 ♕a3 mate) 29 ... ♕c8+ 30 ♔b2 ♕c2+ 31 ♔a3 ♕a4+ 32 ♔b2 ♕xa2+ 33 ♔c1 ♕c2 mate. Readers will not be surprised to discover that this variation was pointed out by the computer program Fritz. To the human eye 28 ... ♘b4+ appears to give White's king too many options to escape in comparison with 28 ... ♕xa2+ which reduces the alternatives.

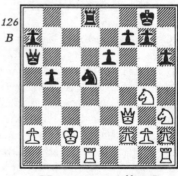

126
B

28 ...   ♕xa2+
29 ♔d3   ♕c4+
White resigns

Black now has a forced mate in seven moves. After 30 ♔d2 ♘b4+ 31 ♕d5 (if 31 ♔e3 or 31 ♔e1, 31 ... ♘c2 is checkmate) 31 ... ♖xd5+ 32 ♔e3 ♖d3+ 33 ♖xd3 ♕xd3+ 34 ♔f4 ♘d5+ 35 ♔e5 ♕c3+ 36 ♔d6 ♕c7 checkmate.

7   Vladimir Kramnik

Player's Name: Vladimir Kramnik
Date of Birth: 25 June 1975
Nationality: Russian
Main Strengths
Powerful attacker, well versed in theory. Exhibited great talent at an early age. Cool and self-possessed in critical situations.
Main Weaknesses
Lacks quality of supreme persistence. Occasionally experiences problems with concentration and dedication.

It is extraordinary that so many of the world's top players start their names with the letter K. Kasparov, Karpov, formerly Korchnoi, Kamsky and Kramnik. Kramnik has been identified by Kasparov, no less, as a likely future champion. Unlike many of his contemporaries, who lead an ascetic, monk-like existence, avoiding smoking, drinking and late nights, Kramnik appears to be determined to enjoy himself. Recent results indicate that his policy of hedonism is paying off just as handsomely as the puritanical devotion to duty adopted by Gata Kamsky.

In 1927 a group of mind sports visionaries in London put together the very first chess olympics. Teams were invited from all over the world and in fact the British players had one of their best ever results, coming in third. Since then the olympic tournament has expanded enormously. In 1992 in Manila, the capital of the Philippines, and home town of Florencio Campomanes, President of the World Chess Federation, no less than 112 national teams assembled to compete for the medals. The chess movement is now so vast that only FIFA, the governing body for world football, can boast more members.

Before the olympics I questioned whether England, with its team of Short, Speelman, Adams, Nunn, Chandler and Hodgson would find their habitual silver medals threatened by the sudden proliferation of states that had gone to make up the former Soviet Union. In this strongest ever chess olympics the Russian team had inherited Garry Kasparov from the USSR, but stars such as Beliavsky, Vaganian, Azmaiparashvili and Ivanchuk were scattered amongst new teams from Armenia, Azerbaijan, Georgia, Kyrgyzstan, Moldova, Kazakhstan, Turkmenistan, the Ukraine and Uzbekistan. Furthermore Estonia, Latvia and Lithuania (including among their players Shirov, Ehlvest, Shabalov and Oll) were resurrected from the 1939 chess olympiad at Buenos Aires, the last occasion on which they had competed as autonomous states.

Even some foreign teams had been swamped by the exodus of former Soviet grandmasters. The United States, for example, had three former Soviet players in its six-man line-up, with Gata Kamsky, on top board doubtless thirsting for another crack at the world champion. As it was, when Kasparov and Kamsky met in the USA – Russia clash, Kasparov dismissed the younger man with almost contemptuous ease (see the Kasparov section).

The average ratings of the teams were fascinating. Far from being overwhelmed by the flood of former Soviet states England, on paper, still held the number two slot. Russia, despite the seepage of Karpov and Yusupov justified its number one seed with an average World Chess Federation rating of 2645, well into the super-grandmaster bracket. England was in number two slot with 2638, while the USA and the Ukraine were 2629. No other team could average over 2600.

The olympics often proves to be a special observatory for new meteors in the chess firmament. When Karpov dropped out of the Russian team his place was taken by 16-year-old Vladimir Kramnik, a player whom Kasparov himself has predicted as a future world champion and whom Kasparov describes as equal in playing strength to himself when he was sixteen. Here is Kramnik's win from the match against Latvia.

Kramnik – Lanka
Manila Olympiad 1992
King's Indian Defence

1	d4	♘f6
2	c4	g6
3	♘c3	♗g7
4	e4	d6
5	f3	0-0
6	♗e3	♘bd7
7	♕d2	c5
8	d5	♘e5
9	♗g5	♘fd7

10 ♗h6 *(127)*

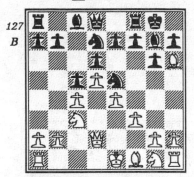

There are some very good rules which urge one to move each piece once in the opening and not more. Here Kramnik breaks that rule since he wishes to exploit Black's time-wasting gyrations with his knights.

10 ... ♗xh6
11 ♕xh6 a6
12 h4

This would also have been the answer to 11 ... f5.

12 ... f6
13 ♕d2

The apparently more vigorous 13 h5 fails to 13 ... g5 when White's queen is shut out of play.

13 ... ♕a5
14 f4 ♘f7
15 ♘f3 ♖b8
16 a4 ♘b6
17 ♗d3 ♗g4
18 ♘h2 ♗d7
19 b3 ♔h8
20 0-0 ♘a8
21 ♕b2 ♖g8

The battle lines are clearly drawn: Black has constructed

what he believes to be a bomb-proof fortress on the kingside while White is angling for a breakthrough in the centre.

22 ♘f3 ♗g4
23 e5 *(128)*

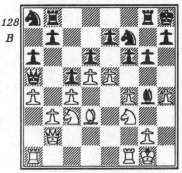

Here Karpov would probably have played 23 ♘h2 followed by ♖ae1 but Kramnik, more in the Kasparov style, now decides to sacrifice a piece to clear a path for his centre pawns.

23 ... ♗xf3
24 exf6 ♗g4
25 fxe7 ♖g7
26 ♘e4 ♘c7
27 ♘f6 ♗h5
28 ♖ae1 ♘e8
29 ♘d7 ♖a8
30 f5 g5
31 hxg5 ♘xg5
32 f6 ♖f7
33 ♗f5 ♘c7
34 ♘f8 *(129)*

A most spectacular position with White's knight having penetrated to Black's first rank. Although Lanka has succeeded in blocking White's dangerous pawns his bishop is so offside that White can win it at his leisure.

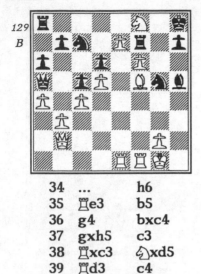

34	...	h6
35	♖e3	b5
36	g4	bxc4
37	gxh5	c3
38	♖xc3	♘xd5
39	♖d3	c4
40	bxc4	♕c5+
41	♕d4	♕xd4+
42	♖xd4	♘e3
43	♗g6	♔g8
44	♖xd6	

Black resigned in view of White's overwhelming material advantage.

Kramnik – Nunn
Manila Olympiad 1992
Kings Indian Defence

1	d4	♘f6
2	c4	g6
3	♘c3	♗g7
4	e4	d6
5	f3	0-0
6	♗e3	c5

This move evidently loses a pawn but of late it has become quite a popular gambit.

7	dxc5	dxc5
8	♕xd8	♖xd8

9	♗xc5	♘c6
10	♗a3	

In Karpov – J. Polgar, Monaco 1993, White preferred 10 ♘d5 (see the section on Karpov).

10	...	a5
11	♖d1	(130)

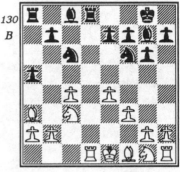

11	...	♗e6

This is John Nunn's attempt to improve on the game Nenashev – Nunn from the match Uzbekistan – England, also from Manila where he played 11 ... ♖xd1+ 12 ♔xd1 ♘b4 13 ♘ge2 b6 and lost in 33 moves.

12	♘d5	♗xd5
13	cxd5	♘b4
14	♗b5	♘c2+

Black appears to be doing well, since he is going to remove one of White's bishops and inflict doubled pawns on the a-file. This would appear to give good value for the pawn.

15	♔f2	♘xa3
16	bxa3	e6 (131)

A curious decision since White now obtains a highly dangerous central passed pawn. However, if Black avoids this course White may consolidate with moves such as ♘e2 and ♖b1 when further weaknesses will appear in the black camp.

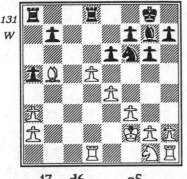

17	d6	e5
18	♘e2	♗f8
19	d7	♗xa3

Black has won back his pawn but White's passed d-pawn is now generating threats of gargantuan dimensions. White's next move inaugurates a kingside attack, while Black is hamstrung on the other wing.

20	g4	h6
21	h4	a4
22	♖d3	♗b2
23	g5	hxg5
24	hxg5	♘h7
25	f4	*(132)*

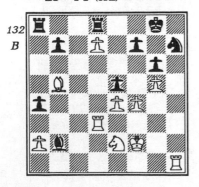

A very fine move. If 25 ... exf4 then 26 ♖d5 followed by ♘xf4.

| 25 | ... | ♖a5 |
| 26 | ♖d5 | f6 |

Black tries to break out of the straitjacket in a different way but falls foul of a sacrifice which creates an overwhelming mass of central pawns, the coronation of at least one of which cannot be prevented.

27	♖xh7	♔xh7
28	gxf6	exf4
29	e5	♔h6
30	♘xf4	♗xe5
31	♖xe5	♖xd7
32	♗xd7	♖xe5
33	f7	

Black resigns

A game of great theoretical importance.

Ivanchuk – Kramnik
Linares 1993

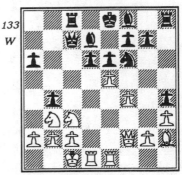

20 ♖d3

A clever idea, but it is refuted even more ingeniously.

20 ... dxe5

21	fxe5	bxc3
22	ℤxc3	*(134)*

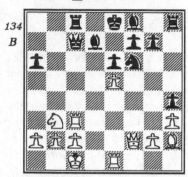

| 22 | ... | ♛xc3 |

An elegant queen sacrifice which drives White's king into the open.

23	bxc3	♗a3+
24	♔d2	♘d5
25	ℤe4	ℤxc3
26	ℤg4	0-0

An example of very late castling.

27	♛xh4	ℤfc8
28	♘d4	♗b4
29	♔e2	♗b5+ *(135)*

The concluding sacrifice which seals White's doom. The final series of forced transactions leaves Black with a decisive material advantage.

30	♘xb5	ℤxc2+
31	♔f3	axb5
32	ℤxb4	♘xb4
33	♛xb4	ℤ8c3+

White resigns

Black will inevitably regain the queen by ... ℤc4+ leaving him with a won endgame.

Yudasin – Kramnik
FIDE Candidates (1),
Wijk aan Zee 1994

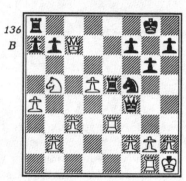

Kramnik played

| 24 | ... | ♛xe3 |

which wins a rook since if 25 fxe3 ♘g3+ 26 hxg3 ℤh5 mate.

25	♘d6	ℤe7
26	♘xf5	gxf5
27	♛d6	♛e5
28	♛b4	ℤae8
29	♛h4	f6
30	h3	♛xd5

White resigns

Beliavsky – Kramnik
Linares 1994
Sicilian Defence

1	e4	c5
2	♘f3	♘c6

3	d4	cxd4
4	♘xd4	♘f6
5	♘c3	d6
6	♗g5	e6
7	♕d2	♗e7
8	0-0-0	0-0
9	f4	♘xd4
10	♕xd4	♕a5
11	♗c4	♗d7 (137)

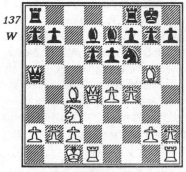

12 ♖he1

One of the most fashionable variations in modern grandmaster chess. In a later round Anand - Beliavsky continued 12 e5 dxe5 13 fxe5 ♘c6 14 ♗d2 ♘d7 15 ♘d5 ♕d8 16 ♘xe7+ ♕xe7 17 ♖he1 ♖fc8 18 ♗f1 with the better game for White. Ironically, Beliavsky lost this later game on the black side.

12	...	♗c6
13	f5	b5
14	♗b3	b4
15	♘e2	♗a4
16	♔b1	

Not 16 fxe6 ♗xb3 17 exf7+ when Black can recapture on f7 with the bishop.

16	...	♗xb3
17	axb3	♖fc8
18	♗d2	♕c7

19	♕d3	exf5
20	exf5	d5
21	♗f4	♗d6
22	g3	a5
23	♗xd6	♕xd6
24	♘f4	a4

Black's strong attack against White's king is of more significance than the weakness of his d-pawn.

25	bxa4	♖xa4
26	♘xd5 (138)	

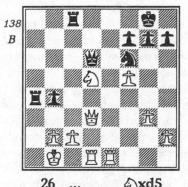

26	...	♘xd5

26 ... ♖ca8 looks crushing since 27 ♘e7+ ♕xe7 28 ♖xe7 ♖a1 is checkmate. However 27 c4 still muddies the waters.

27	♕xd5	♕c7
28	♕e4	♖aa8
29	♖d4	♕a5
30	♔c1	b3
31	c4	♕b4

White resigns

If 32 ♔b1 ♕a4 33 ♔c1 ♖e8 wins.

Over the board Kramnik's presence is immense, as Kasparov found to his cost, when he eliminated him in the following game from their quarter-final clash in the Moscow Speed Chess event. Kramnik's play is characterised by immense energy and a resolve never to shrink from drastic measures when his instinct calls for them.

Kramnik – Kasparov
PCA Speed Chess,
Moscow 1994
King's Indian Defence

The setting for this game, Kramnik's second win against Kasparov within a month, imposingly reflected the importance of a result which may herald the beginning of the end of Kasparov's dominance. An audience of around 3000 knowledgeable spectators followed play on the giant stage of the Palace of Congress Theatre within the walls of the Kremlin in the heart of Moscow. The stage had been set out as a huge chessboard with 20 foot high replicas of the Kremlin's towers and battlements transformed into scarlet and ultramarine chess pieces. Above the players, virtually dwarfed by the arena, was a huge screen with an electronic diagram relaying the moves as they were played. From the start of this game, when the players marched on stage to the strains of Verdi's *Aida*, to its finish, the crowd was enthralled.

1 ♘f3   ♘f6

2 c4   g6
3 ♘c3   ♗g7
4 e4   d6
5 d4   0-0
6 ♗e2   e5
7 d5

The Petrosian variation.

7 ...   ♘bd7
8 ♗e3

Varying from his win against Kasparov in Linares where Kramnik tried 8 ♗g5. The text is most unusual, even bearing in mind the possibility of transposition to similar variations. A check of 150,000 games over the last six years reveals only two games with this variation.

8 ...   ♘g4

Instead 8 ... ♘c5 9 ♘d2 a5, Kuzmin – F. Portisch, Berlin 1988, gives White an easy plus. Black must molest the bishop.

9 ♗g5   f6
10 ♗h4

10 ♗d2 f5 11 ♘g5, Miles – Valesi, Kusadasi 1990 also resulted in a win for White.

10 ...   h5

After the game Nigel Short criticised Kasparov (to his face) for playing this weakening move, recommending instead 10 ... ♘h6. Kasparov responded that he wanted to threaten ... g5, trapping White's bishop. He was scared that, otherwise, White would simply castle kingside with a solid advantage. However, old theory indicates that Kasparov may be mistaken

in this. 10 ... ♘h6 11 ♘d2 g5 12
♗g3 f5 13 exf5 ♘f6 was played
in Mecking – Gligoric, Palma de
Mallorca 1970 and is considered
equal.

11	♘d2	♘h6
12	f3	♘f7
13	♕c2	♗h6
14	0-0-0	*(139)*

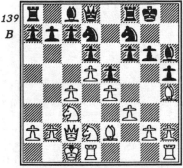

A bold decision indicating
that in the future he will try to
smash Black's kingside with a
storm on the opposite flank.

14 ... c5

Trying to block the position.

15 dxc6

Understandably the young
grandmaster tries to open
things up for an attack. Although this gives tactical chances the strategically superior
method is 15 ♔b1, giving the
option of a slow advance on
either flank, while Black remains cramped.

15	...	bxc6
16	♔b1	a5

After the game Kasparov
criticised himself harshly for
this move, which is really just a
waste of time. Much stronger

is the consolidating manoeuvre
16 ... ♔g7.

17 ♘a4

With the threat of c5, which
Black hastens to prevent, even
though this leaves a hole on d5.

17	...	c5
18	♘c3	♗e3 *(140)*

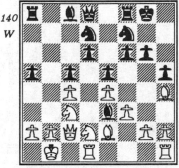

This is quite misguided. It is
normally suicidal to permit the
exchange of the king's bishop
in the King's Indian for a
knight. In this case, Kasparov
even encourages the exchange.

19	♘d5	♗d4
20	♘b3	♗b7
21	♘xd4	cxd4
22	f4	♖b8
23	♖hf1	♘h6
24	c5	

Bold, imaginative but probably premature. Clearly, Black
cannot capture this pawn with
either 24 ... dxc5 or 24 ... ♘xc5
on account of 25 fxe5. Nevertheless Kasparov was more
concerned by the variation 24
g4 hxg4 25 ♖g1 heading directly
for his king.

24	...	♗xd5
25	exd5	♘f5

Here Kasparov looked quite happy with his position. He threatens ... ♘xc5 and ... ♘xh4, so White must sacrifice.

26 fxe5   ♘xh4
27 exd6   ♘e5
28 ♖xd4   ♘f5 *(141)*

141
W

White has a mass of dangerous pawns for his piece but the black knights are sturdy defenders. In order to stoke up the attack White must sacrifice further material, which Kramnik did without hesitation.

29 ♖xf5   gxf5
30 ♕xf5   ♔g7?

Totally overlooking a further sacrifice. As Nigel Short pointed out immediately after the game Black has to play 30 ... ♖b4! to eliminate one of White's most dangerous attacking units. After 31 ♖xb4 axb4 32 ♕e6+ ♔h8 it is possible that the game could end in perpetual check, or Black might even land a counter-punch against the white king. For example 33 ♕e7 ♕c8 34 c6 ♕f5+ 35 ♔a1 ♖f7 36 ♕e8+ ♔g7 37 c7 ♕c2 when White is in

trouble. More sensible for White is 33 ♕xh5, though after 33 ... ♕a5 Black's threat of ... b3 should guarantee him against loss.

31 ♕xh5   ♖h8 *(142)*

142
W

32 ♖g4+!!

As Kramnik hammered out this move, the audience erupted in cheers, thinking that 32 ... ♘xg4 33 ♕g6+ ♔f8 34 ♕f7 checkmate was forced. Kasparov gesticulated wildly at the auditorium, indicating that the game was not yet over, but from now on it proved impossible to quell the spectators' noisy enthusiasm.

32 ...   ♔f8
33 ♕e6 *(143)*

143
B

A lethal quiet move which leaves Black paralysed.

33 ... ♖b7
34 c6 ♖xb2+

Black's last chance. A desperate throw for perpetual check.

35 ♔xb2 ♕b6+
36 ♔a3 ♕c5+

White's king now has to run the gauntlet and it was Kramnik's turn to wave his hands at the audience to prevent their premature jubilation at his anticipated victory.

37 ♔a4 ♕c2+
38 ♔b5 ♕b2+
39 ♔a6 ♕e2+
40 ♔b7 ♖h7+
41 d7 *(144)*

Black resigns

The audience went wild. Not only the official bulletin

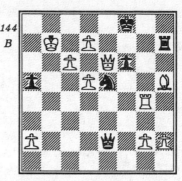

but also several other sources, now gave the further moves "41 ... ♘xc6 42 dxc6 Black resigns". This is, of course, nonsense since Black would win with 42 ... ♕xe6, when White's d7-pawn remains pinned to his own king. Furthermore after 41 ... ♘xc6 42 ♖g8 is checkmate. I watched this game and I can guarantee that those extra moves did not occur.

8 Gata Kamsky

Player's Name: Gata Kamsky
Date of Birth: 2 June 1974
Nationality: American (formerly USSR)

Main Strengths

A fighter - extraordinarily determined and focused on his goal. Dedicated to becoming world champion. Lives for chess.

Main Weaknesses

Some holes in his theoretical preparation. Sometimes nervous. Not tactically at the highest imaginative level.

Gata Kamsky, now the leading US player, defected from the USSR to the United States when he was 15. His father Rustam has always exerted a powerful influence on the son. His training methods are reputedly harsh, but they appear to have been extremely successful. Kamsky is not noted as a profound student of opening theory, nor does his play sparkle with that sacrificial elegance and power of attack which characterises Kasparov. Instead, Kamsky shines by virtue of dogged persistence and an accumulation of small advantages, which he often conducts to victory in exceedingly long games. He seems almost emotionless at the board yet, on occasion, he is capable of conjuring up a violent onslaught, if the preceding stages are susceptible to the workings of pure logic. There is something robotic about his play but, given the opportunity, he can strike with a deadly and flowing efficiency.

**Kamsky - Tal
New York Open 1990**

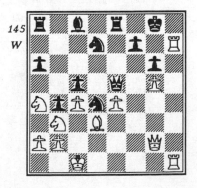
145
W

Having conducted a fierce offensive against the former World Champion, Kamsky now had the chance for a coruscating finale.

26 ♖h8+

This exchange gives White a winning endgame, in the long run, since Black cannot defend his pawns. However, here Kamsky misses a brilliant winning coup, which is very much quicker and considerably more stunning than the move chosen, namely 26 ♘b6!! ♛xb6 27 ♕g3!! deflecting Black's knight to remove the defender of his queen, when Black is helpless against ♖h8+.

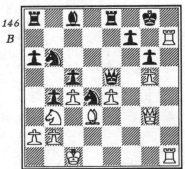

146
B

This reinforces my point that Kamsky's greatest strength is dour determination, not imaginative pyrotechnics.

26	...	♛xh8
27	♖xh8+	♔xh8
28	♘bxc5	♘xc5
29	♘xc5	♘e6
30	♘a4	♗b7
31	♘b6	♖ad8

31 ... ♘c5 32 ♗c2 makes no difference.

32	♘d5	♔g7
33	♕f2	♗xd5
34	♕f6+	♔g8
35	cxd5	♘c5 (147)

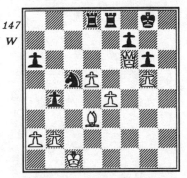

147
W

It is still a safe win, but less impressive than would have been possible on move 26.

36	♔d2	a5
37	♕d4	♘d7
38	♗b5	♖f8
39	e5	♘b8
40	d6	♘d7
41	♔d3	♖fe8

Tal must have been in a dreadful time scramble, uncertain as to whether he had made the moves to the time control at move 40.

42	♗xd7	♖xd7
43	♔e4	♖dd8
44	♔d5	♖b8
45	d7	

Black resigns

**Timman – Kamsky
Alekhine Memorial,
Moscow 1992
Torre Attack**

1	d4	♘f6
2	♘f3	g6

3	♗g5	♗g7
4	c3	d5
5	♘bd2	0-0
6	e3	♘bd7
7	♗e2	♖e8
8	♕b3	c6
9	0-0	e5
10	e4 *(148)*	

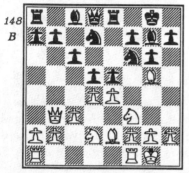

148
B

Timman claims, after his sedate opening, that this move is in the style of Alekhine. Since it comes close to losing, I think he is flattering himself.

10	...	exd4
11	cxd4	dxe4
12	♗c4	

White sacrifices a piece in order to create pressure against the vulnerable pawn on f7. Black could now play 12 ... exf3 but after 13 ♗xf7+ ♔h8 14 ♗xe8 White has considerable pressure. Kamsky defends more accurately.

12	...	♖e7
13	♘xe4	

Spectacularly insisting on sacrificing a piece. 13 ♘e5 is less sensational but it leads nowhere after 13 ... ♕e8.

13	...	♖xe4

14	♗xf7+	♔h8
15	♖ae1	♕f8
16	♘e5	♖xd4
17	f4	♖d5 *(149)*

149
W

A powerful move which returns some material in order to break the force of White's attack. If now 18 ♘xg6+ hxg6 19 ♕h3+ ♘h7 20 ♖e8 ♕xe8 21 ♗xe8 ♘df6 and White's attack dissolves. Also 18 ♗xg6 ♕c5+ 19 ♔h1 ♘xe5 20 fxe5 ♖xe5 21 ♗xf6 ♗xf6 22 ♕f7 fails to 22 ... ♗g7.

18	♗xd5	♘xd5
19	♗e7	

A cute trick. Black cannot take the piece because of a check on f7 with the white knight. However, White's ingenuity can be sidestepped and Kamsky trades off into a favourable endgame.

19	...	♕g8
20	♘xd7	♗xd7
21	♕xb7	♕c8
22	♕xc8+	♖xc8
23	♗c5	a6
24	b3 *(150)*	

It often happens that when a cavalier offensive is repulsed, the attacking party becomes demoralized and slides rapidly downhill. Here, for example, the solid 24 ♖f2, as recommended by Timman after the game, would have been good enough for a draw. By surrendering control of the c3 square to Black's minor pieces Timman facilitates Kamsky's technical task of exploiting his slight material advantage.

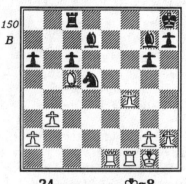

24	...	♔g8
25	♖f2	♗c3
26	♖d1	♖e8
27	h3	♖e4
28	♔h2	h5
29	♖c1	♗e1
30	♖fc2	♘xf4
31	♖c4	♖xc4
32	bxc4	♗g3+ *(151)*

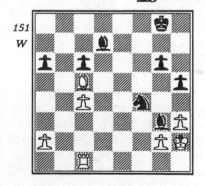

Of course White cannot capture this because of the knight fork on e2.

33	♔h1	♘f5
34	♖c3	h4
35	♖e3	♘d3
36	♗d4	♔f7
37	c5	a5
38	a4	♗e1
39	♖e2	♗b4
40	♗f2	♘xf2+
41	♖xf2	♗xc5

White resigned since Black's bishops will easily shepherd home his passed pawn.

Kamsky (USA) – Kramnik (Russia)
World Team Championship, Lucerne 1993
Semi-Slav

1	d4	d5
2	c4	c6
3	♘c3	♘f6
4	♘f3	e6
5	♗g5	h6

The critical line is 5 ... dxc4 6 e4 b5 7 e5 h6 8 ♗h4 g5 9 ♘xg5 as occurred *inter alia* in the game Kamsky – Shirov from the same event (see the section on Shirov).

6	♗xf6	♕xf6
7	e3	♘d7
8	♗d3	

White enjoys the advantage of greater control of space and more rapid development, while Black's position is solid, and he has the bishop pair.

8 ... g6 *(152)*

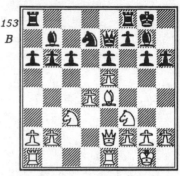

This appears time-wasting, but it is hard to refute. Kramnik envisages a more fruitful future for his king's bishop on g7 than at e7 or d6.

9 0-0 ♗g7
10 e4 dxc4

Instead 10 ... dxe4 11 ♘xe4 ♕f4 12 c5 0-0 13 ♘d6 is quite unpalatable for Black and indicates some of the risks involved in developing the king's bishop to g7, where it depletes the defences of the d6-square.

11 e5

Not 11 ♗xc4 e5 and Black equalizes.

11 ... ♕e7
12 ♗xc4 0-0
13 ♕e2 b6

This appears too slow. Black would do better with 13 ... ♘b6 14 ♗b3 c5. Perhaps Kramnik overlooked White's 16th move in the game.

14 ♖fe1 a6
15 ♗d3 ♗b7
16 ♗e4 *(153)*

The key move to maintain White's advantage. The more natural 16 ♘e4, heading for d6, permits Black to break out with 16 ... c5.

16 ... ♖a7
17 ♖ac1 b5
18 ♕e3 c5
19 d5

This resolute advance is the only way to put severe pressure on Black's position. The complications after 19 dxc5 ♗xe4 20 ♘xe4 ♘xe5 21 ♘xe5 ♗xe5 22 ♕xh6 burn out after 22 ... ♗xb2.

19 ... ♘xe5

This looks risky but if 19 ... exd5 20 ♘xd5 ♗xd5 21 ♗xd5 with the twin threats of e6 and b4. Alternatively 19 ... exd5 20 ♘xd5 ♕e6 21 ♘f4 ♕xa2 22 ♖a1 ♕c4 23 ♗xb7 ♖xb7 24 ♖xa6 also leaves White with a powerful threat of e6.

20 ♘xe5 ♗xe5
21 dxe6

This far-flung pawn represents a permanent health hazard to Black's position. 21 ... ♕xe6 would now shed material after 22 ♗xb7 ♗xc3 23 ♕xc3 while 21 ... fxe6 loses to 22

♕xh6 ♗xc3 23 ♕xg6+ ♗g7 24
♕h7+ ♔f7 25 ♕h5+.

21	...	♗xe4
22	♘xe4	♗xb2
23	♖xc5	♗g7

Again the e6-pawn is im-
mune since 23 ... ♕xe6 fails to
24 ♖c2.

24	♖c6	

Sacrificing a pawn to launch
the final assault.

24	...	fxe6
25	♘c5	♕f7
26	♘xe6	♖e8
27	♕b3	*(154)*

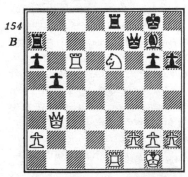

White's knight on e6 is both
dominating and secure, for
example, 27 ... ♖ae7 28 ♖xa6 or
27 ... a5 28 ♕xb5.

27	...	♔h8
28	g3	♕f5
29	♖e2	

The threat is 30 ♘xg7.

29	...	♖ae7
30	♖xa6	♗f6
31	♖e3	♔h7
32	♖f3	♕e5
33	♘f4	♕b2
34	♕d3	

Black's position is falling
apart.

34	...	♖e4
35	♔g2	♕d4
36	♕xb5	♖8e7

Black resigned without
waiting for the lethal 37 ♘d5.

Van der Sterren - Kamsky
FIDE Candidates,
Wijk aan Zee 1994
King's Indian Defence

1	d4	♘f6
2	c4	g6
3	♘c3	♗g7
4	e4	d6
5	♘f3	0-0
6	♗e2	e5
7	♗e3	♘g4
8	♗g5	f6
9	♗c1	*(155)*

White's opening strategy
look strange, having apparently
wasted three moves with his
bishop to return it to its start-
ing square. The justification,
though, is that Black has been
obliged to loosen his kingside
pawn structure and will lose
time in his turn when his
knight on g4 is inevitably

chased back.

9	...	exd4
10	♘xd4	f5
11	0-0	♘c6
12	♘xc6	bxc6
13	exf5	gxf5
14	h3	♘f6
15	♗f3	♗d7
16	♗g5	♖b8
17	♕d2	(156)

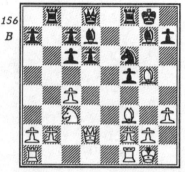

Indeed, the outcome of the opening has favoured White. He has regained his lead in development and Black's pawn structure has more holes than an Emmental cheese.

17	...	♕e8
18	♖ae1	♕f7
19	b3	♔h8
20	♖e2	♖be8
21	♖fe1	♖xe2
22	♖xe2	♘g8
23	♗f4	♘e7
24	c5	

The standard thrust in such situations to undermine the black pawn constellation.

24	...	♘g6
25	♗h5	♗c8 (157)

Of course 25 ... d5 would relieve the pressure against the d6-pawn but leave c7 undefended.

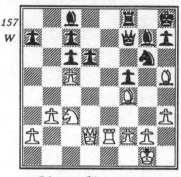

26 cxd6

Impatient to cash in on his advantage the Dutch Grandmaster seizes a hot pawn, always a dangerous thing to do. I would have preferred 26 ♘a4, increasing the pressure. If then 26 ... ♗a6 27 ♖e1 ♗b5 28 cxd6 cxd6 and now White can play 29 ♕xd6 with advantage. Alternatively 26 ... d5 27 ♗xg6 hxg6 28 ♗e5 with a permanent dark-square grip.

26	...	cxd6
27	♗xd6	♖d8
28	♘a4	♕f6
29	♕b4	

The point of White's play. He breaks the pin and ensures the win of a pawn. The danger is that Black's pieces are becoming very active.

29	...	♖xd6
30	♖e8+	♗f8
31	♖xc8	♔g7
32	♕b7+ (158)	

Playing with fire by withdrawing his pieces from the kingside. Both 32 ♕c3, seeking to trade queens, and 32 ♕e1 would have been preferable, and would have maintained White's advantage.

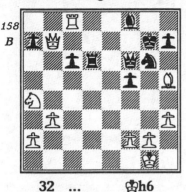

32 ...   ♔h6
33 ♗f3

Now Black's pieces stream out but if White tries to eliminate Black's attacking force with 33 ♗xg6 then 33 ... ♖d1+ 34 ♔h2 ♗d6+ leaves Black in control.

33 ...   ♘h4
34 ♗e2

If 34 ♗xc6 ♖d1+ 35 ♔h2 ♗d6+ 36 g3 ♕d4 wins.

34 ...   ♕a1+
35 ♗f1 *(159)*

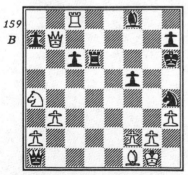

If 35 ♔h2 ♖g6 36 g3 ♕d4 wins.

35 ...   ♘f3+

The final devastating tactic, which turns the wheel full circle.

36 gxf3   ♖g6+
White resigned

37 ♔h2 ♗d6+ forces mate.

Van der Sterren – Kamsky
FIDE Candidates,
Wijk aan Zee 1994
King's Indian Defence

15 ♗xf5

A novel motif, since White must wreck his kingside pawn structure in order to regain the material.

15 ...   ♖xf5
16 g4   ♖f8
17 gxh5   ♕h4

A bold response, leaving his queenside to White's mercy.

18 ♘e4   ♘f6
19 ♘xd6   ♗h3
20 ♖g1   ♖ad8
21 ♖c7   ♗g4 *(161)*

A most extraordinary idea. If now 22 fxg4 ♘xg4 23 ♖xg4 ♕xg4 the advantage passes to Black, while 22 fxg4 ♘xg4 23

♖g2 ♘xe3 24 ♖gxg7 ♖f1+ 25
♕xf1 ♘xf1 26 ♖xh7+ leads to a
draw by perpetual check.

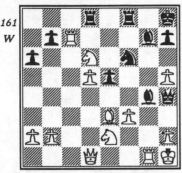

161
W

22	♘c3	♗xh5
23	♖gxg7	♖xd6
24	♗c5	

White's rooks doubled on
the seventh rank appear to be a
terrifying force but it is difficult to land the decisive blow.
For example, if now 24 ♘e4
then 24 ... ♕xe4 25 fxe4 ♗xd1
26 ♗c5 ♖fd8 is an adequate
defence.

| 24 | ... | e4 |
| 25 | ♖g3 *(162)* | |

Apparently a supine with-
drawal but the more adventurous continuation 25 ♗xd6
♗xf3+ 26 ♕xf3 exf3 27 ♗xf8
♕e1+ 28 ♖g1 f2 leads to Black's
advantage.

162
B

25	...	♕f4
26	♗xd6	♕xd6
27	♖xb7	

With his threat of ♕d4
White at last appears to be
getting somewhere but Kamsky's next elegant trick trans-
poses into a level endgame.

| 27 | ... | ♕xg3 |

Black's salvation. In contrast
27 ... ♗xf3+ 28 ♖xf3 exf3 29
♕xf3 leaves Black helpless.

28	hxg3	♗xf3+
29	♔g1	♗xd1
30	♘xd1	♘xd5
31	♖b3	♖c8
32	♘c3	♘xc3
33	♖xc3	♖d8
34	♖e3	♖d2
35	♖xe4	♖xb2
36	♖a4	♖b6
37	♔g2	**Draw**

9   Boris Gelfand

Player's Name: Boris Gelfand
Date of Birth: 24 June 1968
Nationality: Byelorussian
Main Strengths
Well versed in theory, a dangerous and accomplished attacking player. Superbly well trained. Excellent calculator.
Main Weaknesses
Can be derailed by unorthodox play from the opponent. A potential victim of the unexpected.

Boris Gelfand first made his mark at the highest level at the Linares tournament of 1990. Here he not only came second to Kasparov but contested a most thrilling game with the champion, in which the result could have gone either way. At that time, Kasparov predicted that Gelfand was his most likely successor. Since then, though, Gelfand's star has somewhat waned, largely as a result of his drubbing by Nigel Short in the 1991 Candidates Quarter-final. Short mercilessly exposed Gelfand's lack of psychological preparation, expressed in his inability to cope with suddenly changing positions on the board. It also became clear, in the examination conducted by Short, that although Gelfand was an adept in opening systems he had studied deeply, he found it difficult to orientate himself against less orthodox systems.

In recent events, though, Gelfand has once more demonstrated his ambition to reach the top. He won the FIDE Interzonal in 1993 and in the first stage of the FIDE Candidates cycle he eliminated Michael Adams with consummate ease. His style is scientific, but packs a combinative punch when necessary. Against Adams, Gelfand also demonstrated that it is no longer so easy to unnerve him with offbeat systems.

Kasparov managed to stay on top of the category 16 tournament in Linares, Southern

Spain in 1990, but only after he had been given something of a fright by the then 21–year–old Boris Gelfand.

Gelfand won as many games as Kasparov, the high total of 6 and his vigorous, inventive and erudite style reminds me somewhat of the young Kasparov himself.

Linares 1990

Kasparov 8/11; **Gelfand 7½**; Salov 7; Ivanchuk 6½; Short 6; Gulko, Yusupov 5½; Beliavsky 5; Spassky, Illescas, Portisch 4; Ljubojevic 3.

Gelfand – Anand
Biel FIDE Interzonal 1993
Semi–Slav Defence

1	d4	d5
2	c4	c6
3	♘c3	♘f6
4	e3	e6
5	♘f3	♘bd7
6	♗d3	dxc4
7	♗xc4	b5
8	♗d3	♗b7

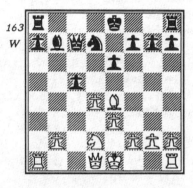

163 W

The more popular alternative is 8 ... a6 but then Karpov – Kramnik from Linares 1994 continued 9 e4 c5 10 d5 c4 11 dxe6 fxe6 12 ♗c2 ♗b7 13 0–0 ♕c7 14 ♘g5 ♘c5 15 e5 ♕xe5 16 ♖e1 with a dangerous attack. In their later game from Monaco Kramnik sought to improve his play by trying 10 ... ♕c7 against Karpov and, in fact, won that game.

9	a3	b4
10	♘e4	♘xe4
11	♗xe4	♕c7
12	axb4	♗xb4+
13	♗d2	♗xd2+
14	♘xd2	c5 *(163)*

The complications of the opening appear to have burnt out and a draw does not seem far off. However, White's coming manoeuvre subtly nudges the black queen away from the defence of the knight on d7.

15	♕c2	♕b6
16	dxc5	♕xc5
17	♕a4	

The point of White's play. The pin against the black knight hamstrings Black's development.

17	...	♖b8
18	0–0	0–0

An ingenious solution. Anand seeks to cut the Gordian knot by sacrificing a piece temporarily.

19	♕xd7	♖fd8
20	♗xh7+!	*(164)*

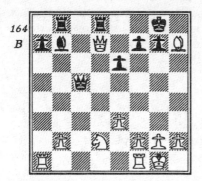

164
B

The only way to try to refute Black's strategem. White sacrifices two pieces back to expose the black king.

20 ...   ♔xh7

This is where Black goes wrong. He should have declined the sacrifice with 20 ... ♔f8 when after 21 ♕a4 ♖xd2 22 ♕xa7 ♕xa7 23 ♖xa7 g6 White's bishop is trapped. Alternatively 22 ♖ac1 ♕d5 23 ♕a3+ ♕d6 leaves White marginally better but Black should be able to hold the draw. The most likely outcome is that White will have to exchange queens and then withdraw his bishop from the exposed h7-square. Black will probably lose his a7-pawn in exchange for White's pawn on b2. In that case, though, White's extra pawn, with all the pawns being on the king-side, ought not to be enough to win.

21 ♕xf7   ♖xd2
22 ♖a4

This sudden and unexpected introduction of hitherto dormant reserves into the battle

swiftly decides the issue.

22 ...   ♕g5
23 g3

The winning move. Black cannot avoid the deadly check on h4 and his queen sacrifice merely staves off inevitable defeat.

23	...	e5
24	♖h4+	♕xh4
25	gxh4	♖d6
26	h5	♗e4
27	♕e7	♖bb6
28	♕xe5	♖e6
29	♕f4	

Black resigns

Gelfand – Shirov
Chalkidiki 1993
Slav Defence

1	d4	d5
2	c4	c6
3	♘c3	♘f6
4	♘f3	a6 *(165)*

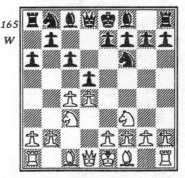

165
W

This innocent-looking pawn move has become high fashion in the Slav. Black speculates on 5 e3 b5 6 b3 ♗g4, which has been extremely successful from the black point of view.

Cvitan - Bareev, played at Tilburg in November 1993, saw 7 h3 ♗xf3 8 gxf3 ♘bd7 9 cxd5 cxd5 10 a4 b4 11 ♘e2 when, after 11 ... e6, Black had the more comfortable position.

5 ♘e5

Clearly a more vigorous way of handling the position. Alternative methods of seeking to profit from Black's unconventional handling of the opening are 5 a4 e6 6 g3 as in Ivanchuk - Shirov, also at Tilburg and 5 c5 g6 6 ♗f4 ♘h5 7 ♗e5 f6 8 ♗g3, as in another Gelfand - Shirov game from Chalkidiki.

5	...	♘bd7
6	cxd5	cxd5
7	♗f4	e6
8	e3	b5
9	♗d3	♗b7

White's light-squared bishop on d3, aiming at Black's king, is far more effective than its black counterpart, hemmed in on b7. In compensation, however, Black has more space on the queenside.

| 10 | 0-0 | ♗e7 |
| 11 | a4 *(166)* | |

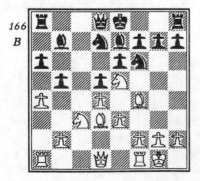

Trying to disturb Black's harmonious queenside development by puncturing his pawn front.

| 11 | ... | b4 |
| 12 | ♘a2 | |

A standard manoeuvre. The knight is heading for c1 in order to re-emerge on the safe square b3, blockading Black's b-pawn.

12	...	0-0
13	♘c1	♘xe5
14	dxe5	

14 ♗xe5 ♘d7 15 ♗g3 ♕b6 promises White very little. The recapture in the text saddles White with doubled pawns but permanently drives away Black's defensive knight from f6 and also opens up the d4-square as a future outpost for White's remaining knight.

14	...	♘d7
15	♘b3	♖c8
16	♕e2	♕b6
17	a5	♕a7
18	♖fc1	♕a8
19	♕h5 *(167)*	

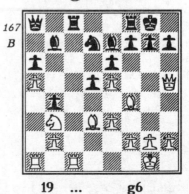

| 19 | ... | g6 |

The storm-clouds are gathering around the black king. Black must weaken his kingside in this fashion for if 19 ... h6 20 ♗xh6 gxh6 21 ♕xh6 f5 22 ♕xe6+ ♖f7 23 ♕xd7 and White wins.

20	♕g4	♖xc1+
21	♖xc1	♖c8
22	♖a1	

A curiously retrograde move in the middle of an attack. Gelfand's plan was evidently to avoid the general exchange of heavy pieces on the c-file, which would have alleviated Black's defensive task. White's problem was to find a good square on the back rank for his rook, while avoiding the trade. The square a1 was chosen, so as to lend extra protection to the a5-pawn, before deciding which would, in fact, be the most useful attacking square. I suspect, though, that Gelfand had overlooked the tactic, three moves away, by which Shirov in any case picks up the white a-pawn.

22	...	♕b8
23	♕g3	♗d8
24	♘d4	♘c5
25	♗b1	

Unfortunately, Gelfand has to lock in his rook if he wants to keep his bishop on the most aggressive diagonal. 25 ♗c2 fails to 25 ... b3 26 ♗xb3 ♗a8 27 ♗c2 ♕xb2 28 ♖b1 ♕c3.

| 25 | ... | ♗xa5 *(168)* |

An unpleasant back-rank trick, for if now 26 ♖xa5 ♘e4 (with the threat of ... ♖c1 mate)

wins.

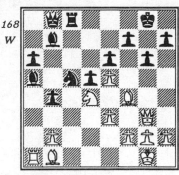

26 h4

Undeterred by the loss of his a-pawn, Gelfand now throws everything into a direct attack against the black king.

26	...	♗d8
27	h5	♕c7
28	♗h6	♕e7

If instead 28 ... ♘e4 then 29 ♗xe4 dxe4 30 hxg6 hxg6 31 ♘xe6 fxe6 32 ♕xg6+ ♔h8 33 ♕xe6 with the idea of ♖d1-d7. This variation shows that White's rook might have been better placed on d1 at move 22.

29	hxg6	hxg6
30	♗xg6 *(169)*	

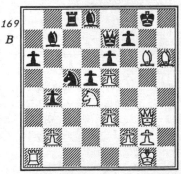

Although the consequences of this sacrifice are not immediately clear, it is obviously White's most promising and consistent choice.

30	...	fxg6
31	♕xg6+	♔h8
32	♖c1	♖c7
33	f4	

Threatening 34 ♗g5.

33	...	♕h7
34	♕e8+	♕g8
35	♗f8	♖f7

35 ... ♗h4 leads to immediate loss as follows: 36 ♖xc5 ♖xc5 37 ♕h5+.

36 ♕xd8 ♘d3

Alternatives also fail, e.g. 36 ... ♕xf8 37 ♕xf8+ ♖xf8 38 ♖xc5 or 36 ... ♖xf8 37 ♕h4+ ♕h7 38 ♕xh7+ ♔xh7 39 ♖xc5. Shirov's choice also loses to a thunderbolt.

37 ♖c7!! (170)

The point is to deflect Black's rook from the defence of f6. If now 37 ... ♖xf8 38 ♕h4+ wins or 37 ... ♕xf8 38 ♕xf8+ ♖xf8 39 ♖xb7 with a winning endgame.

| 37 | ... | ♖xc7 |
| 38 | ♕f6+ | |

The point. Although Black

will temporarily be a rook ahead, he is paralysed.

| 38 | ... | ♖g7 |
| 39 | ♘xe6 | |

In this hopeless position **Black resigned**. 39 ... ♘xb2 40 ♗xg7+ ♔h7 41 ♕h6 checkmate is one possible conclusion.

Gelfand – Adams
FIDE Candidates,
Wijk aan Zee 1994
Queen's Gambit Accepted

1	d4	d5
2	c4	dxc4
3	e3	

Avoiding the traditional 3 ♘f3 Gelfand opts for a variation with a certain 19th century flair to it.

3	...	e5
4	♗xc4	exd4
5	exd4	♘f6
6	♘f3	♗e7
7	0-0	0-0
8	h3	♘c6 (171)

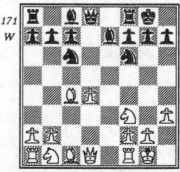

Conventionally Black is not advised to block his c-pawn in this fashion in queenside openings. Instead of this 8 ... c6 9

♗e3 ♘bd7 10 ♗b3 ♘b6 11 ♘c3 ♘fd5 12 a4 a5 13 ♘e5 ♗e6 14 ♗c2 f5 would transpose into the game La Bourdonnais – McDonnell, from one of their great matches at London in 1834. Note that in this game, the ... f5 theme re-emerges on move 15.

9	♘c3	♘a5
10	♗d3	♗e6
11	♖e1	♘c6
12	a3	♕d6

This appears to expose the black queen. Amazingly the game has transposed into the 48th and final game between Kasparov and Karpov from their first championship match which was terminated prematurely in February 1985. That game started life as a Petroff! There Karpov tried ... a6 which, combined with a later ... ♘d5 might well be a preferable means of defence.

13	♗e3	♘d5
14	♕c2	♔h8
15	♖ad1	

Not 15 ♗xh7 g6.

15	...	f5 *(172)*

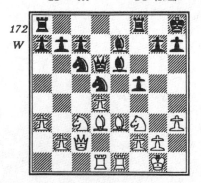

Seeking some kingside activity but this weakens the e-file, shades of La Bourdonnais - McDonnell.

16	♗c1	♖ad8
17	♖e2	♗f6
18	♖de1	♗c8
19	♗c4	♘xc3

Strengthening White's centre but after 19 ... ♘b6, 20 ♘b5! exploits the awkward situation of Black's queen.

20	bxc3	h6
21	a4	b6
22	h4	♘a5
23	♗a2	c5 *(173)*

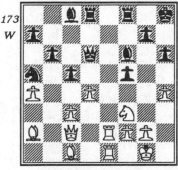

24	♘g5

An annoying stroke which gains valuable terrain. After 24 ... hxg5 25 hxg5 Black's bishop is trapped and his king is exposed.

24	...	♗a6
25	♖e6	♕d7
26	♕xf5	

This amounts to a winning sacrifice and must have come as a terrible surprise to Black. After 26 ... hxg5 27 hxg5 White has the added threat of ♕h3+. However, what Black plays is little better.

26	...	♗xg5
27	♕g6	

The point of White's play. 27 ... ♗xc1 fails to 28 ♖e7 while 27 ... ♗xh4 loses to 28 ♘b1 ♗xf2+ 29 ♔h1 ♔g8 30 ♕h7+ ♔f7 31 ♗g6 checkmate. Black decides, instead, to try to defend a lost endgame.

27	...	♕f7
28	♕xf7	♖xf7
29	hxg5	cxd4
30	cxd4	

Safe enough, but 30 gxh6 might have been even more devastating.

30	...	♗c4
31	♖e8+	♖xe8
32	♖xe8+	♔h7
33	♘b1+	g6
34	gxh6	♘c6
35	♗e3	♖e7
36	♖c8	♗d5
37	♗d3	♘b4
38	♗e2	♗e6
39	♖d8	♘d5 (174)

With two extra pawns and the bishop pair White's task is not difficult.

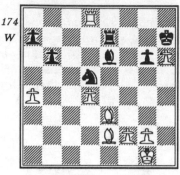

174
W

40	♗g5	♖d7
41	♖e8	♗f7
42	♖b8	♗e6
43	♗f3	♖f7
44	♖d8	♖f5
45	♗d2	♘f6
46	♖a8	g5
47	♖xa7+	♔xh6
48	♖a6	♘d7
49	a5	♖b5
50	axb6	

Black resigns

If 50 ... ♘xb6 51 ♗a5 wins a piece while if 50 ... ♖xb6 51 ♖a5 nets a further pawn.

10 Vassily Ivanchuk

Player's Name: Vassily Ivanchuk
Date of Birth: 18 March 1969
Nationality: Ukrainian
Main Strengths
Superbly accomplished theoretician, attacker and strategic player.
A huge talent.
Main Weaknesses
Inordinately nervous, lacking in self-confidence and prone to panic
in a crisis.

In 1991, at the start of the year, Vassily Ivanchuk, clearly and convincingly won what had been billed by the Spanish organizers as the strongest tournament ever held until that time. In so doing, Ivanchuk achieved the hitherto unique double of beating both Karpov and Kasparov in the same tournament, and he also crushed Kasparov's decade-long record of finishing no lower than first equal in every important tournament in which he had participated. Apologists for the World Champion may well point out that their man would have been tired after his exertions in the recently-concluded World Championship match. It should be stressed, though, that Kasparov actually performed up to his 2800 rating in Linares, and it was Ivanchuk who surpassed all expectations.

Linares 1991
Ivanchuk 9½/13; Kasparov 9; Beliavsky 8; Yusupov, Speelman 7½; Salov 7; Timman, Karpov 6½; Ljubojevic, Anand, M. Gurevich 6; Gelfand 5½; Ehlvest 3½; Kamsky 2½.

Ivanchuk – Gelfand					
Linares 1991			2	c4	g6
Grünfeld Defence			3	♘f3	♗g7
1	d4	♘f6	4	g3	0-0
			5	♗g2	d5

6	0-0	dxc4
7	♘a3 *(175)*	

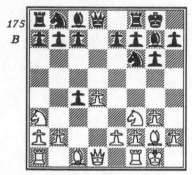

175
B

A variation well known to theory but regarded by aficionados of the Grünfeld as fairly harmless for Black. White acquires a considerable pawn centre, but it is felt that Black can generate plenty of counterplay with his active pieces and fianchettoed king's bishop.

7	...	c3
8	bxc3	c5
9	e3	♘c6
10	♕e2	♕a5
11	♗b2	♘d5

This crude attack against c3 clearly looks somewhat suspect, since Black's knights lack stable posts in the centre of the board. Evidently preferable is 11 ... ♗f5 12 ♖fc1 ♗e4 as in Adorjan - Kindermann, Altensteig 1989.

12	♖ac1	b6 *(176)*

If Black's previous handling of this opening was unwise, then this move, which fulfils the doubly disastrous function of cutting off the retreat of his queen and exposing Black to pressure from the white bishop on g2 towards the black knight on c6 and the rook on a8, must be classed as downright foolish.

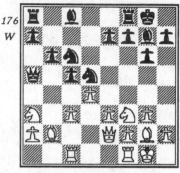

176
W

13	♘d2!	

A superb move, unmasking the full force of the fianchettoed king's bishop, whilst simultaneously threatening to transfer his knight to the queenside to bring the black queen *in angustis*.

13	...	e6
14	♘b3	♕a6
15	c4	♘db4
16	♘b5	♕a4
17	♘c3	♕a6
18	a3 *(177)*	

Black resigns

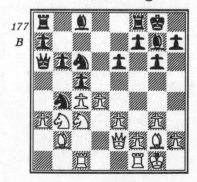

177
B

Black loses at least a piece for absolutely no compensation. A sensationally swift win against a powerful opponent.

Ivanchuk – Short
Novi Sad Olympiad 1992
USSR – England

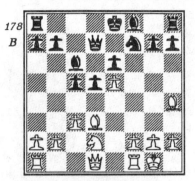

The opening has been an unusual variation of the French Defence. Short now decides that his main priority is to castle his king into safety on the queenside. Indeed, the greedy capture 13 ... ♘xe5 would expose Black to a dangerous attack after 14 ♕h5+.

13	...	♗e7
14	♗xe7	♕xe7
15	f4	0-0-0
16	♕e2	♔b8
17	♖ae1	g6
18	a3	c4
19	♗c2	♕c5+
20	♕f2 *(179)*	

A mature decision. Many chess enthusiasts mistakenly believe that trading queens must automatically lead to a boring position. This is not true

and Ivanchuk here espies his chances in the endgame.

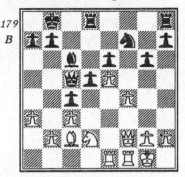

20	...	d4
21	♗e4	

Sensibly blunting the power of the black bishop.

21	...	♘h6
22	cxd4	♕xd4
23	♘f3	♕xf2+
24	♖xf2	♖c8
25	♗xc6	♖xc6
26	♖d2	♘f5
27	♘g5	h5
28	♔f2	♖e8
29	h3 *(180)*	

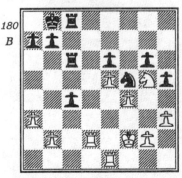

Although Black's position is riddled with a number of pawn weaknesses there is absolutely no need to panic. The correct course now is 29 ... h4! to paralyse White's potentially mobile mass of pawns on the kingside. Thereafter Black can operate with threats such as ... c3 to open more files for his rooks. After the strategic blunder of the text Black is swiftly swamped.

29	...	b6?
30	g4	hxg4
31	hxg4	♘g7

After this abject retreat Black's position becomes resignable. His knight is totally crippled and he has weak pawns everywhere. Short had probably been relying in his initial calculations on seeking salvation with 31 ... ♘h6 overlooking that White can then win with 32 ♖h1 ♘xg4+ 33 ♔f3 trapping the knight.

32	♖h1	c3
33	bxc3	♖xc3
34	♖h7	♖c7
35	♖h6	♖f8
36	♔e3	a6
37	♖xg6	(181)

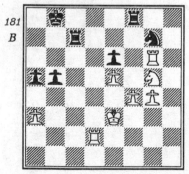

181 B

The harvest begins.

| 37 | ... | ♖h8 |
| 38 | ♘xe6 | ♘xe6 |

39	♖xe6	♖c3+
40	♔e4	♖g3
41	♖xb6+	

Black resigns

**Ivanchuk – Anand
Linares Match,
Game 7, 1992
Sicilian Defence**

1	e4	c5
2	♘f3	d6
3	d4	cxd4
4	♘xd4	♘f6
5	♘c3	♘c6
6	♗g5	e6
7	♕d2	♗e7
8	0-0-0	0-0
9	f4	♘xd4

Preparing to enter a line which is rapidly becoming the height of fashion.

10	♕xd4	♕a5
11	♗c4	♗d7
12	e5	

For 12 ♖he1 see Beliavsky – Kramnik in the Kramnik section.

| 12 | ... | dxe5 |
| 13 | fxe5 | (182) |

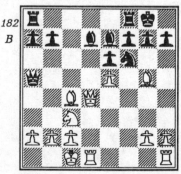

182 B

This is a well-known variation of the Richter–Rauzer

Sicilian. White appears to be winning material but Black's next move saves the day, due to the vulnerability of White's bishop on g5.

13	...	♗c6
14	♗d2	♘d7
15	♘d5	♕c5
16	♘xe7+	♕xe7
17	♖he1	

So, White has gained the advantage of the bishop pair but Black's position remains resilient.

17	...	♖fd8
18	♕g4	♘f8
19	♗d3 *(183)*	

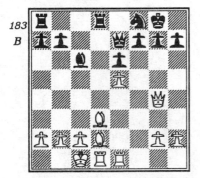

183 B

White's bishops look dangerous, but Black's next move, sacrificing the exchange, gives him excellent counterplay.

19	...	♖xd3
20	cxd3	♕d7
21	♔b1	

Amazingly, this is the first new move of the game. 21 ♗b4 was tried in Psakhis - Greenfeld, Tel Aviv 1991 and 21 ♖e3 in Ivanov - Rachels, US Championship 1989. White tempts Black to take the pawn on d3

with check.

21 ... ♕xd3+

Considering the further course of the game this looks like an error, but in fact this move is not the real source of Black's problems. Nevertheless, Black could instead consider 21 ... ♗d5 followed by an advance on the queenside.

22 ♔a1 *(184)*

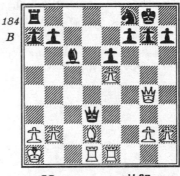

184 B

22 ... ♕f5

Black could now have justified his previous move with 22 ... h5!! when after 23 ♕xh5 ♗a4! or 23 ♕e2 ♕g6! Black's position is fairly solid. As played, Black's queen raid has simply captured an unimportant pawn, driven the white king into safety and opened up lines for White's rooks.

23	♕g3	♘g6
24	♗c3	h6
25	♖f1	♕e4
26	♖d2	♗d5
27	b3	♖c8
28	♔b2	a6
29	♖df2	♖c7
30	♖e1	♕h4
31	♕xh4	♘xh4 *(185)*

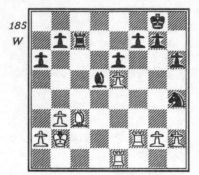

185
W

Anand still has some compensation but he has failed to achieve the aim of the variation, which is to sacrifice the exchange for the initiative and an attack on the queenside.

32	♖d1	♘g6
33	g3	♘e7
34	♖d4	♘c6
35	♖df4	♖d7
36	h4	h5
37	g4	hxg4
38	♖xg4	♘e7
39	h5	♗c6
40	h6	♘g6
41	hxg7	♔xg7
42	♗b4	♗d5
43	♗d6	b6
44	a4	b5
45	a5	f5 *(186)*

186
W

Anand loses patience and also the game. His position was already uncomfortable because of the weakness on a6 but this hands Ivanchuk the point on a plate.

46	exf6+	♔f7
47	♗e7	e5
48	♖h2	♘xe7
49	fxe7	♔xe7
50	♖g6	e4
51	♖xa6	

Black resigns

Georgiev – Ivanchuk
Tilburg 1993
Sicilian Defence

1	e4	c5
2	♘f3	d6
3	d4	cxd4
4	♘xd4	♘f6
5	♘c3	a6

White's next move is in fashion again. It had been Fischer's favourite in the 1960s.

6	♗c4	e6
7	♗b3	b5
8	0–0	♗e7
9	♕f3	♕c7
10	♕g3	♘c6 *(187)*

187
W

Offering the same sacrifice of his g-pawn which Kasparov tried against Short in game 16 of their match in London 1993.

11	♘xc6	♕xc6
12	♖e1	♗b7
13	♕xg7	

Considerably more prudent would be 13 a3 ♖d8 14 f3 0-0 15 ♗h6 ♘e8 16 ♔h1 Short - Kasparov, World Championship, Game 16, a game which Nigel Short went on to win, though he could hardly claim any advantage from the opening duel - see section on Short.

13	...	♖g8
14	♕h6	0-0-0

It is not often in the Najdorf Variation of the Sicilian Defence, that Black has the opportunity to castle queenside and launch a vigorous assault down the g-file. A curious parallel, however, was the game Nikitin - Tal, Tbilisi 1959 which had gone 1 e4 c5 2 ♘f3 d6 3 d4 cxd4 4 ♘xd4 ♘f6 5 ♘c3 a6 6 ♗g5 ♘bd7 7 ♗c4 ♕a5 8 ♕d2 e6 9 0-0 h6 10 ♗h4 ♗e7 11 ♖ae1 ♘e5 12 ♗b3 g5 13 ♗g3 ♗d7 14 f4 gxf4 15 ♗xf4 ♕c7 16 ♘f3 0-0-0 17 ♔h1 ♖hg8 18 ♗e3 ♗c6 19 ♕d4 ♖g6 20 ♖e2 ♖dg8 and Tal ultimately won. The comparison is rendered even more piquant by the fact that for many years Nikitin was the coach of none other than Garry Kasparov.

15	♕h3	♔b8
16	f3	♖g6

17	a3	♖dg8
18	♖e2	h5

The advance of this wing pawn is designed to ignite the residence of the white king.

19	♔h1	♕c7

Commencing a remarkable manoeuvre to increase his influence over the kingside.

20	♘d1	h4
21	♘e3	♘h5
22	♘g4	♕d8 *(188)*

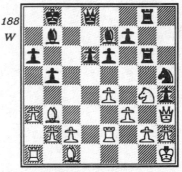

188
W

The culmination of Ivanchuk's idea. He plans to play ... ♗g5 to control f4. Black would like to hurl in ... f5, to rupture White's central zone, but at the moment the activity of White's bishop on b3 precludes this possibility.

23	♗d2	♗g5
24	g3	

In seeking to defend f4 from alien invasion White allows a blow to develop from another angle.

24	...	f5

Now this is sound, since White dare not open the diagonal of Black's lurking bishop on b7.

25	♘e3	fxe4
26	f4	♗xf4
27	♗xe6	

Of course 27 gxf4 ♘xf4 is murderous but the text also meets with a crushing refutation which emphasizes Black's domination of the open g-file.

27	...	♖xg3
28	hxg3	♘xg3+
29	♔g2	♘xe2+
30	♗xg8	♕xg8+
31	♔f2	♘d4
32	♘f5	

White seeks to confuse the issue, but Ivanchuk has everything under control.

32	...	♗xd2
33	♘xd4	e3+
34	♔f1	♕c4+

White resigns

After 35 ♘e2 ♕f7+ 36 ♔g1 ♕f2 is checkmate. A sparkling orchestration of a grand original theme.

Ivanchuk – Kasparov
Amsterdam 1994
Sicilian Defence

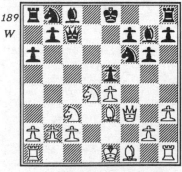

189
W

11 ♗h6!!

A stunning tactical coup which is easy to overlook. The point of Ivanchuk's idea is that if now 11 ... 0–0 12 ♗xg7 ♔xg7 13 ♕xf6+ ♔xf6 14 ♘d5+ ♔g7 15 ♘xc7 winning on material.

11	...	♗xh6
12	♕xf6	

With White's queen so aggressively placed, and the looming threat of ♘d5, Black risks suffering an opening debacle.

12	...	0–0
13	♘d5	♕a5+
14	b4	

Kasparov's next move relinquishes his queen for two minor pieces and generally inadequate compensation. The big question must be, why did he not play instead 14 ... ♗g7? The best I can find for White in that case is 15 ♕xg7+ ♔xg7 16 bxa5 exd4 17 ♘b6 ♖a7. In this position Black is inconvenienced by the displacement of his rook but in compensation White's a5-pawn is also weak. Black may stand worse but he is far from lost. Incidentally after 14 ... ♗g7 if 15 bxa5 at once 15 ... ♗xf6 16 ♘xf6+ ♔g7 when White has nothing better than transposition to a position similar to the previous note with 17 ♘d5 exd4 18 ♘b6.

14	...	♕d8
15	♘e7+	♕xe7
16	♕xe7	exd4
17	♗c4	

and White won easily.

11 Alexei Shirov

Player's Name: Alexei Shirov
Date of Birth: 4 July 1972
Nationality: Latvian
Main Strengths
Love of complications, glories in both attack and defence if situation sufficiently complex. Well prepared in chosen openings.
Main Weaknesses
Doubts surround his competitive temperament in a cut-and-thrust qualifying race.

"Some talk of Alexander, and some of Hercules; of Hector and Lysander, and such great names as these;" goes the refrain of the British Grenadiers. Others talk of Gata Kamsky or Anand as the leading lights of the generation which is following Kasparov. But a prospect who should not be overlooked is Alexei Shirov. Being a Latvian, he no longer has the powerful USSR Federation to support him, while his own fledgling Latvian Federation is as yet too feeble to ensure a constant flow of invitations for him to international tournaments. Lone wolf though he is, Shirov has attained an impressive rating.

Here are samples of his play,

which is so daring and unconventional as almost to constitute a new approach to chess strategy. I was particularly struck by his game against Eingorn, during which Shirov conducted a middlegame attack with his own king perched precariously in the centre of the board. I am told by Jon Tisdall that one British Grandmaster had to be helped from the board by his friends after a recent severe defeat at Shirov's hands, such is the violence and physicality of his mode of play.

Efimov – Shirov
Gausdal 1991
Two Knights' Defence

1   e4   e5

2	♘f3	♘c6
3	♗c4	♘f6
4	♘g5	♗c5
5	♗xf7+	♔e7
6	♗d5	♖f8

Anand – Beliavsky, Linares 1991 saw a different plan for Black: 6 ... ♕e8 7 d3 d6 8 ♗xc6 bxc6 9 ♗e3 ♕g6.

7	♖f1	♕e8
8	♘c3	d6
9	h3	♕g6
10	d3	h6
11	♘f3	♕xg2
12	♘h4	*(190)*

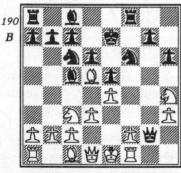

190
B

12	...	♗xf2+
13	♖xf2	♕g1+
14	♖f1	

Or 14 ♔e2 ♘d4+ 15 ♔e3 ♘g4+ 16 hxg4 ♕xf2 mate.

14	...	♕g3+
15	♔d2	♕g5+
		White resigns

Shirov – Ernst
Gausdal 1991
Grünfeld Defence

1	d4	♘f6
2	c4	g6
3	♘c3	d5
4	♘f3	♗g7
5	♗g5	♘e4
6	cxd5	♘xg5
7	♘xg5	c6

Black offers a gambit, but it is more in Shirov's style to offer pawns than to take them.

8	e3	cxd5
9	♕f3	f6
10	♘h3	♗xh3
11	♕xh3	f5
12	g4	

This move heralds a powerful attack on the g-file.

12	...	0-0
13	gxf5	gxf5
14	♖g1	e6
15	♘e2	♖f6
16	♘f4	♘c6
17	♗d3	♕e7
18	♔e2	♖af8
19	♖g5	R8f7
20	♖ag1	♕c7
21	♖h5	*(191)*

191
B

21	...	♘xd4+

The attack reaches its climax and Black acts out of desperation.

22	exd4	♕xf4
23	♖xh7	
		Black resigns

Shirov – Eingorn
Stockholm
Rilton Cup 1989

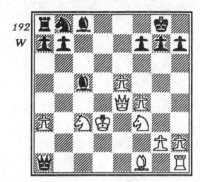

192
W

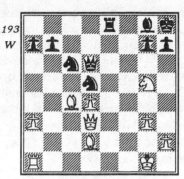

193
W

26	♕xh7+	♘xh7
27	♘f7+	♔g8
28	♘xd6	
	Black resigns	

Black must have believed that he was forcing events, the more so since White's king seems ludicrously exposed on d3. Yet now, with his own king in the very thick of events, Shirov launches the decisive attack.

20	e6	fxe6
21	♘g5	g6
22	♕e5	♗e7
23	♘xe6	♔f7
24	♕g7+	♔e8
25	♘c7+	♔d8
26	♕h8+	♔d7
27	♘xa8	♕xa3
28	♔c2	**Black resigns**

Shirov – Renet
Corréze Match 1991

Black may have thought his position quite secure but White's next thunderbolt swiftly dispels his illusions.

Shirov – Kramnik
Lucerne World Team
Championship 1993
Sicilian Defence

1	e4	c5
2	♘f3	♘c6
3	d4	cxd4
4	♘xd4	♘f6
5	♘c3	d6
6	♗g5	e6
7	♕d2	♗e7

Rapidly becoming one of Black's most reliable defensive systems in contemporary elite chess.

8	0-0-0	0-0
9	f4	♘xd4
10	♕xd4	♕a5
11	♗c4	♗d7
12	♖d3 *(194)*	

12 e5 dxe5 13 fxe5 ♗c6 14 ♗d2 ♘d7 led to a win for White in Ivanchuk – Anand, Linares (match, 7th game) 1992 (see section on Ivanchuk). However,

Black's position out of the opening was satisfactory, hence the novel idea in the text. Shirov's plan is three-fold: extra defence for the knight on c3, increased pressure against the black pawn on d6 and the ability to swing the rook along the third rank into an attack against Black's king.

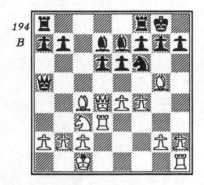

| 12 | ... | e5 |

For a superior method of defence, 12 ... ♖ad8, see Morovic - Leko in the section covering Peter Leko.

13	♕e3	♖ac8
14	♗b3	♗e6
15	♗xe6	exf4
16	♗xf4	

If White greedily tries to keep an extra pawn with 16 ♗xf7+ ♖xf7 17 ♗xf4 then 17 ... ♘g4 18 ♕g3 ♖xf4 19 ♕xf4 ♗g5 wins White's queen. Alternatively 19 ♖d5 ♗g5 20 ♖xa5 ♖f1 is double check and mate.

| 16 | ... | fxe6 |
| 17 | ♕h3 | *(195)* |

Forcing an unpleasant displacement of the black king.

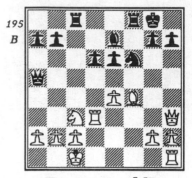

17	...	♔f7
18	♔b1	♕c5
19	g4	h6
20	♗e3	♕e5
21	♗d4	♕g5
22	♖g1	♘d7
23	♗e3	♕g6
24	g5	hxg5

There now follows a temporary piece sacrifice which results in a better ending for White.

25	♗xg5	♗xg5
26	♖xd6	♘c5
27	♕g4	♔g8
28	h4	

White has to avoid the somewhat shallow trap 28 ♕xg5 ♖f1+.

| 28 | ... | ♖f4 |
| 29 | ♕xg5 | |

Now he can recapture on g5 with the h-pawn.

29	...	♕xg5
30	hxg5	♖cf8
31	b4	*(196)*

Amazingly, White can give back the material, but still retains a substantial advantage in the resultant rook and pawn endgame.

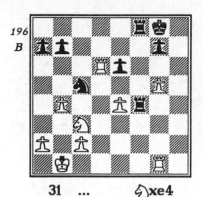

all much too slow.

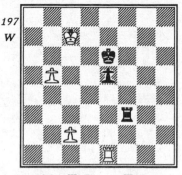

31	...	♞xe4
32	♞xe4	♖xe4
33	a3	♚h7

Black would like to defend his second rank with 33 ... ♖f7 but then 34 g6 is too powerful.

34 ♖d7

It is curious how impotent Black is to prevent the attack against his queenside pawns.

34	...	♚g6
35	♖xb7	a5
36	♚b2	♖f5
37	♚b3	♖e3+
38	♚a4	♖ff3
39	♚xa5	♖xa3+
40	♚b6	♖ac3
41	♖e1	

Here and later White is not concerned with the preservation of his c-pawn. It is the passed b-pawn that will guarantee his victory.

41	...	♚xg5
42	♖xg7+	♚f6
43	♖c7	e5
44	b5	♖xc7
45	♚xc7	♚e6 *(197)*

Kramnik tries to conjure up some last feeble chances with his own passed e-pawn but it is

46	♖e2	♖c3+
47	♚b8	♖c4
48	b6	e4
49	b7	♚d5
50	♖h2	e3
51	♚a7	♖a4+
52	♚b6	♖b4+
53	♚c7	♖c4+
54	♚d7	

Black resigns

If 54 ... ♖b4 55 ♖h5+ ♚c4 56 ♖h4+ ♚c3 57 ♖xb4 and White's pawn queens.

Kamsky – Shirov
World Team Championship,
Lucerne 1993
Semi-Slav Defence

1	d4	d5
2	c4	c6
3	♞c3	♞f6
4	♞f3	e6
5	♗g5	dxc4

In the game Kamsky – Kramnik from the same event Black played the more passive 5 ... h6 (see section on Kamsky). The text invites hair-raising complications and is far more in Shirov's dynamic and highly theoretical style.

6	e4	b5
7	e5	h6
8	♗h4	g5
9	♘xg5	

This variation has been known since the 1940s. White's sacrifice of a piece is purely temporary since he soon regains the material by force.

9	...	hxg5
10	♗xg5	♘bd7
11	exf6	♗b7
12	g3	c5
13	d5	♗h6

An interesting move designed to weaken White's grip over the cramping pawn on f6.

14	♗xh6	♖xh6
15	♕d2	♕xf6 *(198)*

The point of Black's play is that it is now perilous for White to castle kingside. Therefore, if White's monarch flees to the other wing it is moving into a zone where Black has a dangerous preponderance of pawns. The further course of the game illustrates this theme. If White now tries to castle kingside with 16 ♗g2 then there could follow 16 ... ♘e5 17 0-0 0-0-0 18 f4 ♘d3 19 dxe6 ♕d4+ 20 ♔h1 ♖xh2+ 21 ♔xh2 ♖h8+ 22 ♗h3 f5 23 ♘e4 ♗xe4 24 ♕c3 ♘f2 25 ♕xd4 ♖xh3+ 26 ♔g1 cxd4 27 ♔xf2 ♖h2+ 28 ♔e1 ♖xb2 when Black wins.

16	0-0-0	♔f8

Yusupov - Shirov, Linares 1993 saw instead 16 ... ♗xd5 17 ♘xd5 exd5 18 ♗g2 ♘b6 and the game was eventually drawn. The text is more ambitious. Now White should seriously consider 17 g4.

17	f4	♘b6
18	♗g2	exd5
19	♕f2	

The natural recapture on d5 is unfavourable for White, and shows just how disruptive Black's mass of queenside pawns can become, e.g. 19 ♘xd5 ♗xd5 20 ♗xd5 ♖d8 21 ♕g2 c3.

19	...	♖c8
20	♘xb5 *(199)*	

Grabbing a very hot pawn. 20 g4 is probably still equal.

20	...	♘a4
21	♕c2	♕a6
22	♘a3	

If 22 ♘c3 ♘xc3 23 ♕xc3 ♕xa2 24 ♖xd5 ♗xd5 25 ♗xd5 ♖b8.

| 22 | ... | c3 |
| 23 | ♗xd5 | |

If here 23 bxc3 then 23 ... ♕a5 keeps Black's attack on the boil.

| 23 | ... | ♘xb2 |
| 24 | ♕f5 | |

The alternative is 24 ♗xb7, after which follows 24 ... ♕xa3 25 ♗xc8 ♘c4+ 26 ♔b1 ♖b6+ 27 ♔a1 ♕b2+ 28 ♕xb2 cxb2+ 29 ♔b1 ♘a3 checkmate.

| 24 | ... | ♖f6 |
| 25 | ♕h7 | |

If 25 ♗xb7 ♘d3+.

25	...	♕xa3
26	♕h8+	♔e7
27	♖he1+	♔d7
28	♕h3+	♔d6 *(200)*

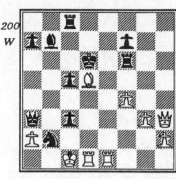

200 W

An amazing position. Black can march his king into a dis-covered check but it is still Shirov's attack which blazes the more fiercely.

29	♗xb7+	♘xd1+
30	♔xd1	♕xa2
31	♕g2	♕b1+

White resigns

After 32 ♔e2 ♖e8+ is spec-tacularly terminal. This extra-ordinarily complicated game deservedly won the brilliancy prize for the tournament.

12 Judit Polgar

Player's Name: Judit Polgar
Date of Birth: 23 July 1976
Nationality: Hungarian
Main Strengths
Brilliantly well prepared, superb tactician and violent attacker. Fearless.
Main Weaknesses
Uncertain in less analysed openings. Somewhat lacking in competitive stamina. Problems with Black, specifically in strategic openings.

Chess has traditionally been a male preserve. But although men dominate the game there is no particular objective intellectual or physiological reason discernible why this should be the case. Nevertheless, it was not until the 1920s, 70 years after the staging of the first international chess tournament, that a female player, Vera Menchik, could make any impression at all on top level chess.

Although Menchik was the strongest woman player in the history of the game, easily outclassing all her other female opponents, she regularly finished near the bottom when competing in male international events. Her main achievement was to notch the scalps of a few isolated male grandmasters such as the one time world champion, Dr. Max Euwe and the British champion Sir George Thomas.

When the Russians began to take over chess after the war all this changed. A school of strong female chess players grew up with a regular world championship match being held every three years. But the new generation of strong women players generally sought glory by defeating each other, in their own restricted female battlefield, rather than venturing out to challenge the men. The breaking of the ice came with the advent of the three remarkable Polgar sisters from Hungary, Judit, Zsuzsa and Sofia. All three of them have terrorized male grandmasters many times their age.

Becoming a chess grandmaster at the age of 15 is the kind of record one does not expect to see broken. At the end of 1991, however, after a gap of more than 30 years Bobby Fischer's record as the youngest ever chess grandmaster was well and truly felled.

Fischer, since 1972, when he won the world championship, had been a virtual recluse. It was in 1958 at the Portoroz interzonal leg of the world championship qualifying competition that Fischer established his record for becoming the world's youngest grandmaster. Fischer was born on March 9th 1943 and on September 10th 1958 he qualified from the interzonal tournament for the world championship candidates competition. This feat automatically made him a grandmaster at the age of 15 years, 6 months and 1 day.

Fischer used to boast that he could cede the odds of a knight to any woman player and still beat her easily. It is, therefore, ironic that it was Judit Polgar, a teenage girl, and the youngest of the three amazing Polgar sisters, who finally smashed Fischer's record. This was a feat, by the way, which has eluded such other modern greats as Kasparov, Karpov, Kamsky, Anand and our own Nigel Short.

Judit Polgar confirmed her grandmaster title in one of most convincing manners possible. Not for her obscure victories against mediocre players in open tournaments but a superb and dominating first prize in one of the strongest ever Hungarian Championships. Hungary, of course, is well-known as a nation with one of the powerful chess traditions, having won the Olympic gold medals on more than one occasion in the past.

Judit Polgar was born on July 23rd 1976 and achieved grandmasterdom on December 20th 1991. Dramatically she saved the best until last, simultaneously earning the title and winning the championship with her victory in the last round game. She therefore became a grandmaster at the age of 15 years, 4 months and 28 days and I will be prepared to bet that Fischer could no longer give her any sort of odds at all and hope to emerge unscathed.

Hungarian Championship 1991

J. Polgar 6/9; Adorjan, Sax 5½; Horvath, Zsu. Polgar 5; Portisch 4½; Lukacs, Groszpeter, Tolnai 3½; Farago 3.

J. Polgar – Groszpeter
Hungarian
Championship 1991
Sicilian Defence

1	e4	c5
2	♘f3	d6
3	d4	cxd4
4	♘xd4	♘f6
5	♘c3	♘c6
6	♗g5	♗d7
7	♕d2	♖c8
8	f4	♘xd4
9	♕xd4	♕a5 (201)

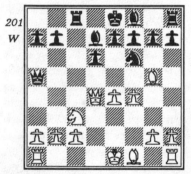

201
W

Black's opening plan looks suicidal, since he encourages White's development and seemingly allows his own mobilized pieces to be chased back. Nevertheless, a number of tactical points come to Black's rescue and the line is considered playable.

10	e5	dxe5
11	fxe5	e6
12	0-0-0	

Here, and on the next move exf6 would be parried by ... ♕xg5. Thus, Black's knight is given time to escape from f6 and Black eludes the worst consequences of his cunctatory mode of development.

12	...	♗c6
13	♗c4	♘d7
14	♖he1	

In contradistinction to Black's somewhat convoluted manoeuvres White's opening strategy is a model of classical clarity and simplicity.

14	...	h6
15	♗d2	♕c5
16	♕f4	

Self-evidently White avoids the exchange of queens since this would eradicate her lead in development.

16	...	g5
17	♕f1	♗g7 (202)

202
W

Black's plan begins to crystallise. He hopes to lay siege to White's exposed pawn on e5, but for this minor success he has to pay a terrible price in terms of the damage inflicted on the integrity of his own kingside pawn constellation.

18	h4	♘xe5

Achieving his goal, even with gain of tempo against White's king's bishop. In any case the alternative 18 ... ♘xg2 19 ♕xg2 ♕xc4 20 ♕xb7 or indeed, 20 hxg5 did not look entirely satisfactory for Black.

19 ♘b3

Nobody likes to accept doubled pawns on the h-file but in fact Black's best defence here is 19 ... gxh4 20 ♘e4 ♘xe4 21 ♖xe4 0-0. As played, Black's pawn on g5 turns out to be a most serious weakness.

19 ...   0-0
20 hxg5   hxg5
21 ♕e2

With typical Polgar directness the queen heads for h5.

21 ...   ♘g6
22 ♕h5   ♕f5
23 g4   ♕f6
24 ♗xg5 *(203)*

24 ...   ♘f4

This loses a piece but already Black's position was far from satisfactory. The last chance to resist, though doubtless a forlorn one, would have been 24 ... ♕f3.

25 ♕h4

Black has no way to keep his queen in contact with his

threatened knight.

25 ...   ♕g6
26 ♗xf4   b5
27 ♕h5   ♕xh5
28 gxh5   a5
29 a3   ♘f3
30 ♖d3   ♗xh5
31 ♖g3   b4
32 axb4   axb4
33 ♘e4   ♘g6
34 ♖xg6

Black resigned in view of 34 ... fxg6 35 ♗xe6+ ♔h7 36 ♖h1+.

The 1992/93 Hastings tournament, the UK's strongest witnessed a remarkable performance by the World's youngest grandmaster. Her share of first prize was the most impressive performance ever achieved by a female player, while her double defeat of Bareev, ranked 8th in the world, was truly extraordinary.

In the final round she trailed Bareev by a full point and had to win to partake of the laurels. She accomplished this in classic style, terminating the victim's resistance with an elegant rook sacrifice. After this triumph, Judit can seriously consider aiming for the supreme world title. With her elder sister Zsuzsa aiming for the women's crown, the day may come when Judit Polgar reigns as absolute world champion while Zsuzsa Polgar is the women's world champion!

Hastings 1992/93
J. Polgar, Bareev **9/14**; Speelman 8; Nunn, Sadler, I. Gurevich 7; Polugaevsky 5½; Crouch 3½.

Here is the more impressive of her two wins over Bareev.

J. Polgar – Bareev
Hastings Premier 1992
French Defence

1	e4	e6
2	d4	d5
3	♘c3	♘f6
4	♗g5	dxe4

This looks passive, but it is a Bareev favourite, often leading, in his hands, to most complicated situations.

5 ♘xe4 ♘bd7

A case in point was Topalov - Bareev, Linares 1994: 5 ... ♗e7 6 ♗xf6 ♗xf6 7 c3 ♘d7 8 ♕c2 e5 9 dxe5 ♘xe5 10 f4 ♘g6 11 g3 0-0 12 ♗d3 ♕d5 13 a3 ♘xf4!! with a dangerous sacrificial attack.

6	♘f3	h6
7	♘xf6+	♘xf6
8	♗e3	♗d6
9	♕d3	b6
10	♘e5	♗b7
11	♕b5+	♘d7
12	0-0-0	a6
13	♕b3	b5
14	c4	0-0
15	f4	♗e4
16	c5	♗e7
17	♗d3	♗xg2

Although this pawn-snatch looks incredibly risky, it is objectively a good move.

18	♖hg1	♗d5
19	♕c2	f5
20	♘g6	♖e8?

This is Black's big mistake, after which he is probably lost. He had to play 20 ... ♖f6! intending to sacrifice rook for knight on g6. One possible line is then 21 c6 ♖xg6! 22 ♖xg6 ♘f8 23 ♖g3 ♗f6 and Black has completely consolidated the kingside and stands well. Now, however, Judit's attack crashes through.

21	c6	♘f8
22	♘e5	♗h4

Black's last chance was 22 ... ♗f6.

23	♕e2	♕f6
24	♕h5	♖ed8
25	♖xg7+!	(204)

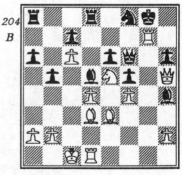

Detonating Black's position.

25	...	♔xg7
26	♖g1+	♔h8
27	♘f7+	♔h7
28	♘xh6	

Black resigns

J. Polgar – Spassky
Match, Budapest 1993
Ruy Lopez

1	e4	e5
2	♘f3	♞c6
3	♗b5	a6
4	♗a4	♞f6
5	0–0	♝e7
6	♖e1	b5
7	♗b3	0–0

A matter of fashion. For some time defending the Ruy Lopez was considered very much a poor second to playing the Sicilian. Now, however, it is all the rage.

8	c3	d6
9	h3	♞b8

Spassky's opening is stuck in a 1970s time warp. The Breyer Variation, introduced with this move, used to be his favourite and was also wheeled out several times against Fischer in their rematch in 1992.

10	d4	♞bd7
11	♞bd2	♝b7
12	♗c2	♖e8
13	♞f1	♝f8
14	♞g3	g6
15	b3	♝g7

Spassky's whole conduct of this game seems too slow and time-wasting. A more active possibility is 15 ... c5.

16	d5	♝f8

A further symptom of Spassky's imperviousness to the dictates of tempi. It is hardly surprising, with this to-ing and fro-ing of the bish-op that White can build up an impressive advantage.

17	♗g5	h6
18	♗e3	c6
19	c4	a5
20	♕d2	♔h7
21	♞h2	*(205)*

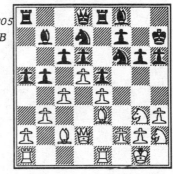

205
B

21	...	b4

It has become a characteristic of Spassky's play with Black to try to block positions and hope that the opponent cannot break through. Here, though, 21 ... a4 would have been more combative.

22	♞g4	♞xg4
23	hxg4	♕h4

At last signs of aggression from Spassky, but this move brings his queen into danger.

24	g5	c5?

The losing move though the refutation was hard to envisage. Black had to play 24 ... cxd5 25 exd5 hxg5 26 ♗xg5 ♗h6 in order to alleviate the pressure.

25	♞f1	

This brilliant retreat in combination with White's imaginative 27th move leaves Black's queen with no sensible path of escape.

25	...	f6
26	g3	♛h3 *(206)*

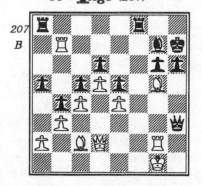

27   f3!!

A superb move, giving up a pawn in order to transfer White's rook into the attack via the second rank.

27	...	fxg5
28	♖e2	♞f6
29	g4	♛xf3
30	♞h2	♛h3
31	♖f1	♞xg4
32	♖f7+	♗g7
33	♞xg4	♛xg4+
34	♖g2	♛h3

If 34 ... ♛c8 35 ♗xg5 wins.

35	♖xb7	♖f8
36	♗xg5 *(207)*	

Giving back the piece to force a decisive attack.

36	...	hxg5
37	♛xg5	♛h6
38	♛xh6+	

The only way to win and of course one does not fall for the snare 38 ♖h2?, met by 38 ... ♖f1+.

38	...	♚xh6
39	♖h2+	♚g5
40	♖xg7	♖f3

Black lost on time but the position is clearly hopeless.

J. Polgar – Rivas
Seville 1993
Pseudo-Philidor

1	e4	d6
2	d4	♞f6
3	♞c3	♞bd7
4	f4	e5

This appears to constitute an entirely novel opening system. It is not covered in any of the standard texts and the earliest example I can find of it dates from 1991.

5	♞f3	exd4
6	♛xd4	c6 *(208)*

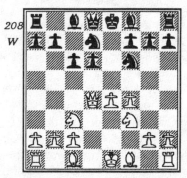

In an earlier round from Seville the game Yudasin – Rivas had now continued 7 e5 dxe5 8 fxe5 ♗c5 9 ♕h4 ♕e7 10 ♗f4 ♗b4 when Black had no difficulty in maintaining the balance.

7 ♗e3 d5

A Promethean attempt to break free of his chains in the centre. The game Schafer – Bocker, France 1991 went instead 8 e5 ♘g4 9 ♗g1 ♘h6 10 0-0-0 ♘c5 11 ♕d2 b5 12 ♘g5 ♖b8 13 ♗xc5 ♗xc5 14 ♘ce4 ♗e7 15 ♕c3 ♖b6 16 ♘d6+ ♗xd6 17 cxd6 0-0 18 ♗d3 with a slight edge to White. Judit tries for more.

8 exd5 ♗c5
9 ♕d3 ♕e7
10 ♘d4 ♘b6

10 ... cxd5 11 0-0-0 simply cedes White a solid advantage.

11 dxc6 *(209)*

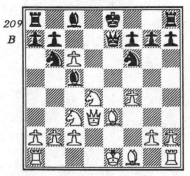

This is the crux of the game. Black has several alternatives to consider, for example from the diagram 11 ... ♘g4, trying to exploit the pin in the e-file. However, White can respond with 12 cxb7 ♘xe3 13 bxa8♕

♘xa8 14 ♔d2. In this line if Black plays 12 ... ♗xb7, which appears to give him a decisive edge in development, then White sneaks out of trouble with 13 ♘f5! ♕c7 14 ♗xc5 ♕xc5 15 0-0-0. Going back to the diagram Black ought to try 11 ... bxc6 hoping for 12 0-0-0 ♗a6! 13 ♕d2 ♗xf1 14 ♖hxf1 ♘c4 15 ♕d3 ♕xe3+ 16 ♕xe3+ ♘xe3 17 ♖fe1 0-0-0 when Black wins. The correct course for White after 11 ... bxc6 is 12 ♗e2 ♗a6 13 ♕d2 ♗xe2 14 ♕xe2 with a good extra pawn, even though Black has some pressure.

11 ... 0-0
12 0-0-0 bxc6
13 ♗g1 ♕c7
14 g3 ♖d8

This is a catastrophic error which overlooks a devastating tactical coup.

15 ♘db5
Black resigns

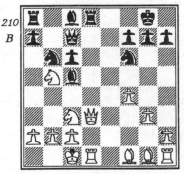

Black's capitulation is absolutely justified. If 15 ... cxb5 16 ♕xd8+ wins on the spot. Alternatively 15 ... ♖xd3 16 ♘xc7 ♖xd1+ 17 ♘xd1 ♗xg1 18 ♘xa8

♞xa8 19 ♖xg1 when White has the exchange and a pawn more and a very easy win.

Khalifman – J. Polgar
Seville 1993

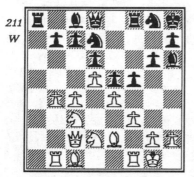

211
W

Judit is clearly a student of Kasparov when it comes to defending against 1 d4. She invariably chooses the King's Indian and has collected some notable scalps with it, including that of Bareev at Hastings. This position represents one of the heavy-duty theoretical lines, the kind of thing you have to know inside out if you want to play it at grandmaster level. Here, for example, an alternative is 16 ♞b5 ♞df6 17 c5 ♞h5 18 ♞c4 ♗d7 19 ♞c3, as in the game Dokhoian – Velikhali, Helsinki 1992.

| 16 | c5 | dxc5 |
| 17 | ♞b5 | |

Another theoretical reference is 17 bxc5 ♞xc5 18 ♞b5 b6 19 ♗b2 ♗g7 20 ♞c4 ♕e7 21 d6 cxd6 22 ♞xb6 as in Illescas – Ivanovic, Manila Interzonal

1990. Judit's database is undoubtedly packed with such references and I am sure that with her prodigious memory she knows all of them. Khalifman is trying to improve on this variation, but he has overlooked a trick.

17	...	c6
18	dxc6	bxc6
19	♞d6	

This looks promising but Judit has everything under control.

19	...	cxb4
20	exf5	♞df6
21	♞xc8	gxf5

This is the point, Black does not need to recapture immediately on c8, since White's knight has no means of escape.

22	♞c4	♗xc1
23	♖fxc1	♖xc8
24	♖xb4	♕d4+

The upshot is, Black has an extra pawn and the initiative.

25	♔h1	♖cd8
26	♖b7	♞h5
27	g3	♖f6 *(212)*

212
W

The threat is now ... ♞xg3+ followed by ... ♕f2.

28	♖g1	♖e8	36	♕e2	♕g7
29	♖bb1	♖h6	37	♔h1	e3
30	♔g2	♖ee6	38	♗h3	♘f2+
31	♗d3	e4	39	♔h2	♖e7
32	fxe4	fxe4	40	♘xe3	♘xd1
33	♗f1	♘hf6	41	♖xd1	♕e5
34	♖d1	♘g4	42	♖d3	♖xh4

The position has turned into a nightmare for White. The queen is, of course, taboo on account of ... ♖xh2 mate.

35	h4	♕f6	43	♕f3	♖h6
			44	♖b3	♖f6
			45	♕g2	h5
			46	♕d2	♖f3

White resigns

At the Madrid tournament the following year, Judith finally demonstrated that she could over-match many of the world's top players. She outdistanced Shirov and Kamsky, amongst others, by an immense margin.

Madrid, May 1994

	1	2	3	4	5	6	7	8	9	10	
1 Polgar	*	1	½	½	1	1	½	½	1	1	7
2 Sokolov	0	*	½	½	½	0	1	1	1	1	5½
3 Illescas	½	½	*	½	½	0	1	1	½	½	5
4 Kamsky	½	½	½	*	½	½	½	1	½	½	5
5 Shirov	0	½	½	½	*	0	½	1	1	1	5
6 Tiviakov	0	1	1	½	1	*	0	0	½	½	4½
7 Salov	½	0	0	½	½	1	*	1	½	½	4½
8 Magem	½	0	0	0	0	1	0	*	1	1	3½
9 SanSegundo	0	0	½	½	0	½	½	0	*	½	2½
10 Bareev	0	0	½	½	0	½	½	0	½	*	2½

13 The Next Generation

Player's Name: Peter Leko
Date of Birth: 8 September 1979
Nationality: Hungarian (with Polgar and Leko, Hungary appears poised to become the chess nation of the 21st century).
Main Strengths
Determined, sharp and well-trained. Youngest ever Grandmaster.
Main Weaknesses
Lacks experience (which will come) and claims himself to be 'lazy!'.

Peter Leko from Hungary has substantially smashed the record for becoming the world's youngest grandmaster. From 1958 until 1991 this had been held by Bobby Fischer. The new record was set by Judit Polgar who on December 20th 1991 became a grandmaster at the age of 15 years 148 days.

At a tournament in Holland Leko pushed down the limit by over a year, becoming a grandmaster at the age of 14 years 145 days.

Here are the full results from the historic event in which Leko smashed the record.

Wijk aan Zee
P. Nikolic 7/9; Tiviakov 5½; **Leko**, Piket, C. Hansen 5; Van Wely, Smirin 4; Morovic, I. Sokolov 3½; Van der Wiel 2½.

In contradistinction to most other successful young players, Leko is a disciple of patient defence and counter-attack, rather than brilliant pyrotechnics. His hero is Petrosian. He aims to be 2700 by 1996 and, of course, wants to break Kaspa-rov's record (22) as youngest world champion!

Morovic – Leko
Wijk aan Zee 1994
Sicilian Defence

1   e4   c5

2	♘f3	d6
3	d4	cxd4
4	♘xd4	♘f6
5	♘c3	♘c6
6	♗g5	e6
7	♕d2	♗e7

Leko has chosen a fashionable variation of the Sicilian Defence, yet one which is rich in counter-attacking possibilities. We have seen it several times already in this book!

8	0-0-0	♘xd4
9	♕xd4	0-0
10	f4	♕a5
11	♗c4	♗d7
12	♖d3	

In Oll – Hodgson from Groningen 1993, White made little progress with the overtly more aggressive 12 e5, which is parried by 12 ... dxe5 13 fxe5 ♗c6.

| 12 | ... | ♖ad8 |
| 13 | ♖g3 | |

White's plan is to bombard the black king with his heavy pieces.

| 13 | ... | ♔h8 |
| 14 | e5 | |

This is the latest attempt to improve on the unproductive 14 ♖f1, as played in the game Shirov – Kramnik, Groningen 1993.

14	...	dxe5
15	fxe5	♗c6
16	♕e3	♘g8
17	h4	

Offering a sacrifice which Black dare not accept. In fact, the grand theme of this game is White's invitation for Black to capture a white piece on g5, but in so doing expose himself to the fury of the suddenly unleashed energy from the white rook on h1.

17	...	♕b6
18	♕e2	h6
19	♗d3	♕d4

Of course, 19 ... hxg5 20 hxg5+ ♘h6 21 gxh6 would give White everything he wants.

20	♖g4	♕c5
21	♗f4	f5
22	exf6	

This looks promising, but 22 ♖g6, refusing to liberate the black position, might have been more accurate. White had clearly been enticed by the opportunities for sacrificial brilliance which now arise.

| 22 | ... | ♘xf6 |
| 23 | ♖g5 | ♕b4 |

Evidently, supine compliance with White's plans, after 23 ... hxg5 24 hxg5+ ♔g8 25 ♕xe6+ ♖f7 26 g6, would be fatal.

| 24 | ♗c7 | ♖xd3 (213) |

A counter-sacrifice to eliminate one of White's most

dangerous units. White must now ponder how to recapture. After 25 ♛xd3 hxg5 26 hxg5+ ♚g8 27 gxf6 ♗xf6 28 ♘d6 White wins. Therefore after 25 ♛xd3 Black must play the more complicated 25 ... ♘g4 (as pointed out by the computer program Fritz), which threatens ... ♘f2 as well as increasing the attack against White's rook on g5.

25 cxd3 hxg5

At last Black can take the ambitious white rook.

26 hxg5+ ♘h7
27 g6

After this White's attacking prospects evaporate, but if instead 27 ♛h5 ♗xg5+ 28 ♛xg5 ♖f1+ 29 ♖xf1 ♘xg5 and Black wins. Perhaps White had overlooked this diabolical trick when initially embarking on his sacrificial adventure.

27 ... ♗g5+
28 ♚b1 ♗h6
29 gxh7 ♛e7
30 ♗e5 ♛g5
31 a3 ♚xh7 *(214)*

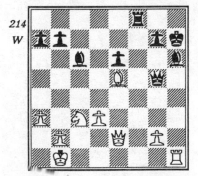

Black has survived the on-slaught and consolidated. With his wide-ranging bishops, and White's weak pawns, Black's advantage is now manifest.

32 ♗d6 ♖d8
33 ♛xe6 ♛g6
34 ♛xg6+ ♚xg6
35 ♗e5 ♖xd3

The resultant endgame is hopeless for White. As so often in the Sicilian Defence, if Black emerges unscathed from White's middlegame attack, he tends to triumph in the ending.

36 ♖e1 ♗xg2
37 ♘b5 a6
38 ♘d6 ♖d2
39 ♘c4 ♖f2
40 ♗g3 ♖f1 *(215)*

The final simplification, which guarantees Black an easy win, with his extra and unstoppable passed pawn.

41 ♖xf1 ♗xf1
42 ♘d6 ♗g2
43 ♗e5 ♗g5
44 ♚c2 ♗f6
45 ♗h2 ♚h5
46 b4 ♗c6
47 ♚d3 b5
48 ♗g1 g5

49	♕d4	♗xd4
50	♔xd4	g4
51	♘f5	♗d7
52	♘e7	♔h4
53	♔e5	♔h3

White resigns

Leko's result in the tournament where he earned the title was not spectacular, consisting mainly of draws with a couple of wins and one loss interspersed against a strong average field. Indeed, his whole style seems somewhat defensively orientated, clearly a disciple of Quintus Fabius Maximus rather than Alexander the Great or, in chess terms, an adherent of Smyslov or Petrosian rather the pyrotechnics of Alekhine or Kasparov. Clearly, though, Leko's result was an extraordinary one, even taking into account the inflation, since Fischer's day in ratings which has made grandmaster norms and high rating performances somewhat easier to achieve.

What struck me most about Leko was that he stormed to two of the three grandmaster performances necessary for the title when only 13, and there was somewhat of a hiatus in his clocking up the third norm. One actually felt that he could have clinched the grandmaster title while still 13, had he put his mind to it. In contrast to the Polgar sisters, proud of their Stakhanovite

credentials, Leko has even gone on record, claiming to be personally lazy. Can it all be sheer talent? Somehow I doubt it, as the highly theoretical opening of the following game demonstrates. This win was crucial in Leko's quest for the title.

Sokolov - Leko
Wijk aan Zee 1994
Grünfeld Defence

1	d4	♘f6
2	c4	g6
3	♘c3	d5
4	cxd5	♘xd5
5	e4	♘xc3
6	bxc3	♗g7
7	♗b5+	

Introducing a fashionable line of the Grünfeld.

7	...	c6
8	♗a4	b5
9	♗b3	b4

Black pursues his theme of undermining White's central installations, the standard strategy in this hypermodern defence.

10 ♗b2

Other sharp alternatives are 10 ♗e3 as in Georgadze - Adorjan, Debrecen 1992 and 10 ♕f3 from Kramnik - Adorjan in the same event.

10	...	bxc3
11	♗xc3	♘d7

A curious alternative is 11 ... ♗a6 12 h4 as in Soppe - Neverov, Cuba 1991.

12 ♘e2

This to me seems stereo-typed, borrowed unthinkingly from the main lines where the development of the knight on e2 is usually obligatory. Here I see nothing to speak against the more active development of White's knight with 12 ♘f3.

12	...	0-0
13	0-0	♗a6
14	♖c1	♖c8
15	♖e1	e5
16	♗b4	♖e8
17	d5	c5

The respective passed pawns cancel each other out.

| 18 | ♗d2 | ♘b6 |
| 19 | ♗e3 | ♗f8 *(216)* |

20 ♗a4

I find this decision hard to understand. Sokolov's plan must have been to increase his attack against Black's split queenside pawns, but now Black's queen's bishop sinks itself into the white camp, while in the further course of play White finds it difficult to capture Black's a-pawn without repercussions. The immediate 20 f3 would have been more

sensible, to firm up his centre.

20	...	♘xa4
21	♕xa4	♗d3
22	f3	c4
23	♘c3	

Had White captured on a7 at any previous stage the reply ... ♖a8 would have been most annoying.

| 23 | ... | a5 *(217)* |

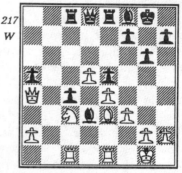

Removing the pawn from danger at long last.

24 a3

This weakens the b3-square and seems unnecessary, since ... ♗b4 was hardly a threat.

| 24 | ... | ♖b8 |
| 25 | ♘d1 | ♖b3 |

Black has taken prompt action and now wins White's a-pawn.

26	♘f2	♖xa3
27	♕c6	♕a8
28	♕f6	♗g7
29	♕h4	♕a6
30	♘g4	♕d6
31	♗h6	

Having lost the battle on the queenside Sokolov transfers his forces into an opportunistic attack against the black king.

31	...	f6
32	♗xg7	♔xg7
33	♕h6+	♔g8
34	♖e3	♖b3
35	h4	♕f8

Precisely timed. White cannot now avoid the exchange of queens which considerably deflates his offensive.

36	♕xf8+	♖xf8
37	♘f2	a4
38	♘xd3	cxd3
39	♖d1 *(218)*	

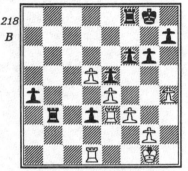

Regaining his pawn but Leko has accurately calculated that the endgame is in his favour.

39	...	a3
40	♖exd3	♖xd3
41	♖xd3	♖a8
42	♖d1	a2
43	♖a1	♔f7
44	♔f2	♔e7
45	♔e2	♔d6
46	♔d3	f5
47	♔c3	fxe4
48	fxe4	♖a3+ *(219)*

Now everything is clear. Black cannot preserve his passed pawn but instead will polish off the weak pawns that constitute the remains of the white camp.

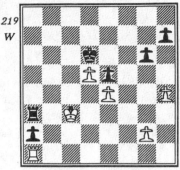

49	♔b2	♖e3
50	♖xa2	♖xe4
51	♖a6+	♔xd5
52	g3	♖c4
53	h5	gxh5
54	♖h6	♖c7
55	♖xh5	♔d4
56	g4	e4
57	♖f5	e3
58	♖f8	e2

The winning move. It will be a simple matter for the black king to shelter on White's first rank in preparation for this pawn's coronation.

59	♖e8	♔d3
60	♖d8+	♔e3
61	♖e8+	♔f2
62	♖f8+	♔e1
63	♔b3	♔d1
64	♖d8+	♔c1
65	♖e8	♖c2

White resigns

Leko – J. Horvath
Budapest 1993
Petroff Defence

1	e4	e5
2	♘f3	♘f6

3	d4	♘xe4
4	♗d3	d5
5	♘xe5	♘d7
6	♘xd7	♗xd7
7	0-0	♕h4
8	c4	♘f6

An interesting attempt to improve on a fashionable variation of the Petroff Defence. In recent games 8 ... 0-0-0 9 c5 has led to White's advantage.

9	♕e2+	♗e7
10	cxd5	♘xd5
11	♗e4	♗c6
12	♘c3	0-0-0

This is much too risky. Correct is 12 ... ♘xc3 13 ♗xc6+ bxc6 14 bxc3 0-0. In that case Black's doubled pawns would not constitute a weakness, whereas in the game they represent an irreparable breach in the king's defences.

13	♕f3	♘xc3
14	♗xc6	(220)

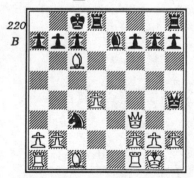

220
B

If now 14 ... bxc6 15 bxc3 ♕f6 16 ♕d3 ♗b7 17 ♖b1+ ♔a8 18 ♗g5 ♕xg5 19 ♕a6 forcing checkmate.

14	...	♘e2+
15	♕xe2	bxc6

16	♗e3	♖d6
17	♖ac1	♖g6
18	g3	♕e4
19	♕a6+	♔d7

Black's position is clearly tottering and one last dagger-stroke will terminate resistance. This is not long in coming.

20	d5	cxd5

Capturing with the queen loses to 21 ♖fd1.

21	♕b5+	♔c8
22	♗xa7	♗d6?

Demoralized by the sudden turn of events Horvath blunders away a rook but if 22 ... ♗d8 23 ♖fd1 ♖d6 24 ♗c5 with a decisive attack.

23	♕b8+	♔d7
24	♕xh8	

Black resigns

Leko - Wells
Budapest 1993
Ruy Lopez

1	e4	e5
2	♘f3	♘c6
3	♗b5	a6
4	♗a4	♘f6
5	0-0	♗e7
6	♖e1	b5
7	♗b3	d6
8	c3	0-0
9	h3	♘b8

The Breyer Variation, made popular, as we have seen, through its adoption by Boris Spassky.

10	d4	♘bd7
11	♘bd2	♗b7

12	♗c2	♖e8
13	a4	♘f8
14	♗d3	c6
15	b3 *(221)*	

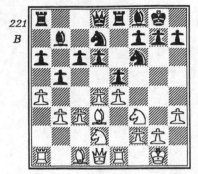

A more aggressive alternative is 15 b4 ♘b6 16 a5 ♘bd7 17 ♗b2. With the text, Leko shows that he is quite content to play a waiting game.

15	...	g6
16	♕c2	♖c8
17	♗b2	♗g7
18	♗f1	♘h5
19	c4	exd4
20	♘xd4	b4
21	♖ad1	c5

The British IM tries to seize the initiative with this thrust. A more patient course would be 21 ... ♘c5.

22	♘e2	♘e5
23	f4	♘d3

A neat coup which gains the bishop pair, for if 24 ♗xg7 ♘xe1.

24	♕xd3	♗xb2
25	g4	♘g7
26	♕c2	♗f6
27	g5	♗xg5 *(222)*

A bold sacrifice, clearly intended when Black played his 23rd move. Black obtains two pawns and some attack for his sacrificed piece. Too passive, on the other hand, is 27 ... ♗e7 28 ♕d3.

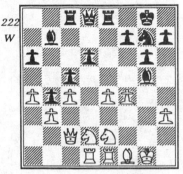

28	fxg5	♕xg5+
29	♗g2	♘f5

Of course this knight cannot be captured.

30	♕d3	♘e3
31	♘g3	♘xd1
32	♖xd1	f5

Wells conducts his attack with commendable élan but here, and on move 45, he suffers a rush of blood to the head. Instead, 32 ... ♖e6 would have been satisfactory, maintaining some pressure, whilst also having material equivalent, in the shape of rook and two pawns, for White's minor pieces.

33	♔h2	f4
34	♘h1	♕e5
35	♔g1	♖cd8
36	♘f2	♕g5
37	♘f3	

White gradually unravels and the minor pieces begin to tell against the rook.

37	...	♛e7
38	♖e1	♛g7
39	h4	h6
40	♔h2	♝c6
41	♖g1	♔h8
42	♝h3	♛c3
43	♞d2	♔h7
44	♝f1	♖e6
45	♖g4	f3 *(223)*

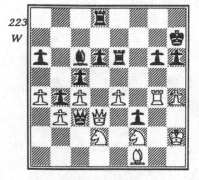

This is suicide. 45 ... ♖f8 still leaves Black in the game.

46	♞xf3	♖f8
47	♔g2	♖ef6
48	♖g3	♖f4
49	♛xd6	

The threat of 50 ♛xg6+ leaves Black little choice. He must now play 49 ... ♖4f6 though after 50 ♛d3 Black is getting nowhere.

| 49 | ... | ♛xf3+ |

This final fling results in an even speedier loss.

50	♖xf3	♖xf3
51	♞g4	♖xf1
52	♛xc6	h5
53	♞e5	♖8f2+
54	♔g3	

Black resigns

Here we leave the games of a possible future world champion and move on to Britain's Great White Hope for 21st century chess glory.

Player's Name: Luke McShane
Date of Birth: 7 January 1984
Nationality: British
Main Strengths
Good in his chosen openings (Sicilian and King's Indian); likes to attack and has a fine feel for the initiative. World's youngest player to obtain a rating, at Lloyds Bank Masters, London 1993.
Main Weaknesses
No consistent experience against top grandmasters, obviously, and dislikes defending.

Kuliev – McShane
World Under-10
Championship,
Duisberg 1992
King's Indian Defence

1	d4	♞f6
2	c4	g6
3	♞c3	♝g7
4	e4	d6
5	f3	0-0
6	♝e3	c5

We have already seen this gambit on several earlier occasions in this book.

7	dxc5	dxc5
8	♗xc5	♘c6
9	♗e2?	*(224)*

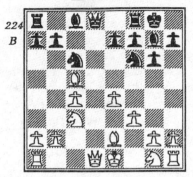

224
B

aison. Black wins back his pawn by this temporary sacrifice and wrecks White's position into the bargain.

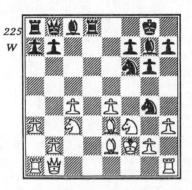

225
W

This move is the root cause of all White's further troubles. If anything, it hinders his own development. The correct procedure is 9 ♕xd8 transposing to the games Kramnik – Nunn (see Kramnik section) and Karpov–Polgar in the essay on Karpov.

9	...	♕a5
10	♗e3	♘b4
11	a3	♖d8
12	♕b1	♘c6
13	♔f2	♕e5

There is clearly something seriously wrong with a white opening which leaves his king and queen so badly misplaced after just 13 moves.

| 14 | f4 | ♕b8 |

In contrast, Black's queen is full of energy on b8.

15	h3	e5
16	fxe5	♘xe5
17	♘f3	♘eg4+

Capablanca would have called this *une petite combin-*

18	hxg4	♘xg4+
19	♔g1	♘xe3
20	♕c1	♘g4
21	♘d5	♗f8
22	♕g5	♕d6
23	♕h4	h5
24	♖d1	♕c5+
25	♔f1	♖xd5

In the style of Kasparov. If White recaptures on d5, then 26 ... ♘e3+ is fatal.

26	b4	♖xd1+
27	♗xd1	♕xc4+
28	♗e2	♕xe4
29	♘e1	♗e6
30	♗f3	♕e3
31	♗xb7	♗c4+

White resigns

McShane – Smallbone
County Match 1993

Here is another quite amazing finish by the ten year old. Luke opened his attack with:

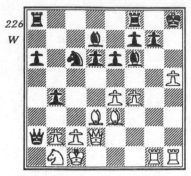

226
W

| 23 | e5 | dxe5 |
| 24 | ⊒g6 | exf4 |

If Black accepts the sacrifice with 24 ... fxg6 then 25 hxg6+ ♔g8 26 ⊒h8+ ♔xh8 27 ♕h2+ ♘h4 28 ♕xh4+ ♔g8 29 ♕h7 checkmate.

25	⊒xf6	gxf6
26	♘d4	e5
27	♕xf4	

Black resigns

For if 27 ... exf4 28 ♘xf6+ ♔g8 29 ⊒g1 checkmate.

Earlier, I discussed the achievement of 14-year-old Peter Leko in becoming the world's youngest ever grandmaster. In the process Leko shaved a year off the previous record of 15, which had initially been held by Bobby Fischer, and then somewhat improved by Judit Polgar. Should one be surprised at this continual lowering of the age for chess stardom? Perhaps not.

With the proliferation of opportunities for formal tournament chess over the past few years, brilliant achievement by youngsters is now easier to register officially. In the past, tournaments were far less common and titles, such as master and grandmaster, were not awarded by established bodies. Is it possible that such prodigies as Paul Morphy, José Capablanca and Samuel Reshevsky might, in fact, have actually achieved what is now recognized as modern grandmaster status, at an even earlier age? After all, Mozart was giving public performances when he was six, and he went on to compose a perfectly competent symphony within a further two years. Perhaps this kind of prodigious achievement is really down to sufficiently early recognition of a young person's drive to take up chess, or indeed music. Given that recognition, the next step is to train appropriately and to find sufficient opportunities to display the respective skill. As things are going, I would not bet against an eight-year-old grandmaster in years to come.

In any case, the French are now also hot on the trail of Peter Leko. 11-year-old Etienne Bacrot has recently scored 50% in the grandmaster tournament at Nice. If anything, he was let down by his stamina, since he had been leading with three points after three rounds but faded towards the end of the competition. Here are two samples of his play.

Santo-Roman – Bacrot
Nice 1994
Sicilian Defence

1	e4	c5
2	♘f3	d6
3	c3	♘f6
4	♗e2	

Setting a crude trap, namely 4 ... ♘xe4?? 5 ♕a4+ winning the knight. One does not have to be a chess prodigy to see through this transparent snare.

4	...	♘bd7
5	d3	b6
6	♘g5	(227)

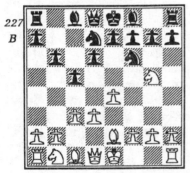

227
B

Another tricky move in the same vein as his fourth. White speculates on a quick win after 6 ... h6?? 7 ♘e6 fxe6 8 ♗h5+ ♘xh5 9 ♕xh5+ with a speedy mate.

6	...	e6
7	f4	h6
8	♘h3	c4

A bold concept, indicating that the 11-year-old is full of confidence in his strategic judgement. Nevertheless, trad-

ing his c-pawn for White's central e-pawn in this fashion does involve a certain loss of time, which compensates White for his arcane gyrations with his king's knight. Objectively, the simple 8 ... ♗b7 might have been more prudent.

9	dxc4	♘xe4
10	0-0	♗b7
11	♘f3	♗e7
12	♖e1	♘df6
13	♘d2	♘c5
14	♗xb7	♘xb7
15	f5	(228)

228
B

In spite of his artificial opening strategy, White has emerged with a fully playable position, based on his control of the central light squares.

15	...	e5
16	♘e4	♕d7
17	♘xf6+	♗xf6
18	♕f3	0-0-0
19	♗e3	♔c7
20	♖ad1	♕c6
21	♕xc6+	♔xc6
22	♖d5	♘a5
23	b3	♔c7
24	♘f2	♘c6 (229)

White's next move, doubtless the product of extreme time pressure, is a gross blunder which loses a pawn. After the superior 25 g4 there is still all to play for.

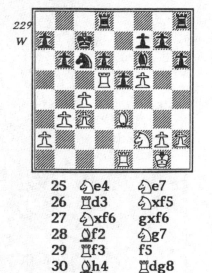

25	♘e4	♘e7
26	♖d3	♘xf5
27	♘xf6	gxf6
28	♗f2	♘g7
29	♖f3	f5
30	♗h4	♖dg8
31	♗f6	f4
32	b4	

This is irrelevant. White had to play 32 g3 to undermine Black's pawn on f4.

32	...	♔c6
33	♖d3	♖h7
34	♖ed1	♘f5
35	♗e7	♖g6 *(230)*

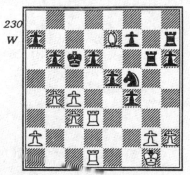

The last difficult move of the game and one which renders White's further resistance futile. Of course not 35 ... ♘xe7 36 ♖xd6+ ♔c7 37 ♖d7+ when White regains the piece.

36	c5	bxc5
37	bxc5	♔xc5

Avoiding the simple pitfall 37 ... ♘xe7 38 cxd6.

38	♖d5+	♔c6
39	♗d8	♘e3

White resigns

The hallmark of Bacrot's play is mature strategic manoeuvring, much in the style of Peter Leko. His knowledge of theory does not appear to be highly developed as yet but he does seem remarkably good at consolidation and the refutation of premature attacks. As further evidence for this assessment of his skills, I join his game against Anic just as Black sets a diabolical ambush.

Bacrot – Anic
Nice 1994

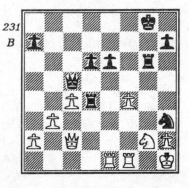

32	...	♖d3
33	f5!	

Bacrot returns his extra pawn in the interests of breaking up the opposing pawn constellation and effecting an advantageous simplification. In the process he avoids the capture 33 ♕xd3 which would have been promptly annihilated by the thunderbolt 33 ... ♕g1+ 34 ♖xg1 ♘f2 checkmate, a device exploiting the otherwise offside placement of the black knight on h3.

232
B

33	...	exf5
34	♕e2	♕c6
35	♕e8+	♕xe8
36	♖xe8+	♔f7
37	♖e3	♖xe3
38	♘xe3	f4
39	♘g2	♖f6
40	♖f3	*(232)*

Bacrot's plan has gone like clockwork. At every stage a forced exchange has underlined the weaknesses in the black camp. Now White wins a pawn, but even then the win requires some technical finesse.

40	...	♘g5
41	♖xf4	♘f3
42	♖xf6+	♔xf6
43	♘e3	♔e5
44	♘d5	a5
45	♘e7	♘d4
46	♔g2	♔e4
47	♔f2	♔d3
48	♘c8	♔c3
49	♘xd6	♔b2
50	♔e3	♘c6
51	♔d2	♔xa2
52	♔c3	♘e5
53	c5	h5
54	♘c4	

Black resigns

Black capitulated on account of 54 ... ♘c6 55 ♘xa5 ♘xa5 56 b4.

14 Deep Thought/Deep Blue

Player's Name: Deep Thought/Deep Blue
Date of "Birth": 1986
Nationality: American
Main Strengths
Tactically outstanding, brilliant calculator and never tires.
Main Weaknesses
Lack of strategic foresight and rather primitive opening theory.

There is a general, if erroneous, fear that computers have already become the true champions in chess. In Brian Appleyard's fascinating book, *Understanding The Present* he writes of efforts to program computers: "Early attempts were held back by the assumption that the computer had to be able to work out every possible future variation from each position ... gradually the problem was overcome by building in horizons of possibility beyond which the computer did not calculate, as well as ways in which it would analyse situations in general rather than in grinding detail. Now computers are as good as the best human players."

Computers may be good at chess, but they are not yet that good!

**Kasparov – Deep Thought
New York 1989,
Exhibition match**

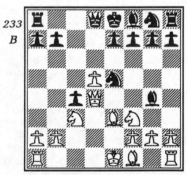

233
B

Deep Thought, in common with most computers, likes to grab material but its following pawn raid, at a severe cost in mobilization, is ill-advised.

10	...	♘xf3+
11	gxf3	♗xf3
12	♗xc4	♕d6
13	♘b5	♕f6
14	♕c5	♕b6

If 14 ... ♘xh1 15 ♘c7+ ♔d8 16 ♘xa8 when Black is completely helpless.

15 ♕a3   e6
16 ♘c7+

This neat coup obliges the silicon monster to surrender its queen, after which further resistance is useless.

16 ...   ♕xc7
17 ♗b5+ ♕c6
18 ♗xc6+ bxc6
19 ♗c5   ♗xc5

Once again, the computer can grab White's rook on h1, but if 19 ... ♗xh1 White wins easily with 20 ♗xf8, with the threat of ♗xg7.

20 ♕xf3 ♗b4+
21 ♔e2   cxd5
22 ♕g4   ♗e7
23 ♖hc1 ♔f8
24 ♖c7   ♗d6
25 ♖b7   ♘f6
26 ♕a4   a5
27 ♖c1   h6 (234)

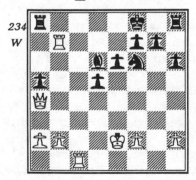

234
W

Black's cause is beyond good and evil.

28 ♖c6   ♘e8
29 b4   ♗xh2
30 bxa5 ♔g8

31 ♕b4   ♗d6
32 ♖xd6 ♘xd6
33 ♖b8+ ♖xb8
34 ♕xb8+ ♔h7
35 ♕xd6 ♖c8
36 a4   ♖c4
37 ♕d7

Black resigns

While Europe's top chess champions and grandmasters, amongst them Garry Kasparov and Nigel Short, gathered in Hungary for the European Team Championship in November 1992, another, very different type of chess championship got under way on the other side of Europe. Indeed, the competition in Madrid, the World Chess Championship exclusively for computers, was packed with boffins whose prime ambition was to seize the championship from the human grandmasters and supplant them with calculating machines.

From November 22nd until November 27th a large hall of the School of Informatics in Madrid University, was lined with computer terminals. Each terminal was adorned with the national flags of the UK, USA, Russia, Germany, France, Holland, Spain (and a host of other nations) all armed with varying programs, each capable of playing chess up to master strength and, in one or two cases, beyond. Some programs had been designed for microprocessors, dedicated solely to playing chess; others were intended to run on PCs, while a minority, such as Hitech from the University of Pittsburgh, were linked to giant mainframe computers, whirring out their checkered calculations from home bases in the US.

The human mastermind behind this Frankensteinian enterprise in the Spanish capital, was International Master David Levy, President of the World Computer Chess Association. The winner at Madrid with 4.5/5 was "ChessMachine Schroeder" written by a wiry-bearded Dutchman of around 50 years, Ed Schroeder from Deventer. He was a popular winner, and if Snow White had been befriended by eight dwarves, instead of seven, he would have fitted in well as "Brainy". *En route* Schroeder defeated the program of the British Professor, Richard Lang who, in the past, had dominated the championship for micro-computers. Lang's program in Madrid, "Chess Genius", was however, afflicted by a bug which robbed it of several well-deserved victories by last-minute howlers. Normally, one associates chess machines with iron logic, but if this was method, there was madness in it. At one moment, Chess Genius was a whole bishop ahead, with an easy win, but

the bug refused to allow it to cash in on its advantage by trading queens (the only way to win and obvious to a human). The inconsolable Lang could only stand on the sidelines, wringing his hands in frustration, as his machine inexorably converted a cast-iron win into a total draw.

The notable absentee from Madrid was the world's most powerful mainframe computer "Deep Thought", recently re-christened "Deep Blue", funded by IBM and based at the Thomas J. Watson Research Centre, Yorktown Heights in New York State. Deep Thought can currently see one million moves per second, but even that colossal calculating ability was, as we have seen, unable to save it when it challenged Garry Kasparov to a two-game match in 1989. Kasparov smashed the machine 2–0 and afterwards said humiliatingly "The main thing Deep Thought needs to learn is when to resign".

In a fit of macho pride and an attempt to restore their self-confidence, Deep Thought team leader, Professor Feng Hsiung-Hsu (known as "Crazy Bird" in the computer world, which happens to be the English translation of his name) announced in 1990 in *Scientific American* magazine that by 1995 Deep Thought would be able to see three billion positions per second and that Kasparov would consequently be "dead meat". Sponsors IBM spotted the article and consequently held Crazy Bird to his word. When asked to explain Deep Thought's absence from Madrid, David Levy said: "The Deep Thought team is working furiously to produce the next generation of the special chess chip which is the core of their hardware. They dare not leave the lab for a minute, they are under such time pressure. It is widely believed that IBM will cut their funding if they do not make significant progress and show some improved results. They are all racing to beat the deadline."

Here is the crucial phase of the decisive last round game from Madrid.

"Kasparov Sparc" – "ChessMachine Schroeder" Computer World Chess Championship, Madrid, 1992

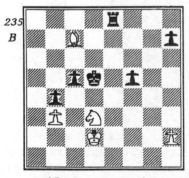

235
B

42 ...   c4

Black tries to create a second passed pawn on the queenside.

```
43  ♘xb4+   ♚c5
44  ♚c3     ♖e3+
45  ♚d2
```

A clever defence but the Black machine now comes up with a masterstroke.

```
45  ...      ♖f3!!
```

A brilliant move and much stronger than 45 ... ♖xb3.

```
46  ♘c2     cxb3 (236)
```

236
W

As a result of its finesse on the previous move the Black machine now obtains two distant passed pawns which prove too much for White's resources to handle.

```
47  ♘a3     ♚d5
48  ♕b6     f4
49  ♕a7     ♚e4
50  ♚c1     ♖h3
51  ♘b1     ♚d3
52  ♚b2     ♖xh2+
53  ♚xb3    f3
54  ♘a3     f2
55  ♕xf2    ♖xf2
    White resigns
```

In spite of its loss to Kasparov, Deep Thought has taken a couple of giant steps for machine-kind. In December 1989 Deep Thought polished off David Levy by the score of four games to zero in the Infolink Challenge at the British Computer Society headquarters in London. More significantly though, in a game played at Harvard, Deep Thought nearly avoided defeat against no less than Anatoly Karpov.

Karpov – Deep Thought
Harvard University, 1990

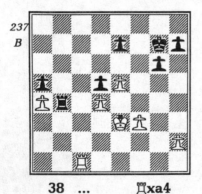

38 ...   ♖xa4

Deep Thought has defended itself with great skill and fully deserves to hold the draw, which it could now have done easily with 38 ... ♖b3+ 39 ♔e2 ♖b4.

39	♖c5	e6
40	♖c7+	♔g8
41	♖e7	♖a3+
42	♔f4	♖d3
43	♖xe6	♖xd4+
44	♔g5	♔f7
45	♖a6	*(238)*

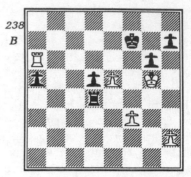

Here there was a trivially easy draw for the machine with 45 ... h6+ 46 ♔xh6 ♖h4+ 47 ♔g5 ♖h5+ 48 ♔f4 ♖f5+ and ... ♖xe5.

45	...	a4
46	f4	h6+
47	♔g4	♖c4

47 ... g5 was the final chance to draw.

48	h4	♖d4
49	♖f6+	♔g7
50	♖a6	♔f7
51	h5	gxh5+
52	♔f5	♔g7
53	♖a7+	♔f8
54	e6	♖e4
55	♖d7	♖c4
56	♖xd5	h4
57	♖d3	♔e7
58	♖d7+	♔f8
59	♖h7	h5
60	♔e5	h3
61	f5	♔g8
62	♖xh5	a3
63	♖xh3	a2
64	♖a3	♖c5+
65	♔f6	

Black resigns

A mathematical point for Karpov – but a moral victory for Deep Thought.

Conclusion

So what is the future destination of the chess crown? Will Kasparov equal, or improve on, Lasker's record of holding the title for almost 27 years? That would mean stepping down in 2012! When Kasparov is eventually defeated, or retires, will his place be taken by one of the Old Masters, Fischer or Karpov, reclaiming their ancient thrones, or will the sceptre pass to the younger generation, perhaps even the first female world champion? Or is the future of chess to be domination by machines, as appears increasingly the case with chess's sister game, draughts?

I think it is likely that, by the year 2000, computers will increasingly face Grandmasters on level terms, but it may well be a further decade before they seriously threaten the human world champion.

And who will that champion be? If not Kasparov, my money is on Anand, Kramnik or, if he maintains his fabulous curve of success, Peter Leko.

Table of Results

The following table charts the results from games played between the players in this book. The list includes all games played in international competitions, including speed chess games played at the time limit of 25 minutes or more per player.

Apart from young players with no games against the main group, the only player missing from the list is Bobby Fischer. In the last twenty years he has only played against Spassky.

	Karpov			Short			Anand			Adams			Kramnik		
	+	=	–	+	=	–	+	=	–	+	=	–	+	=	–
Kasparov	26	117	20	21	17	4	5	2	3	1	0	0	1	3	2

	Kamsky			Gelfand			Ivanchuk			Shirov			Polgar		
	+	=	–	+	=	–	+	=	–	+	=	–	+	=	–
Kasparov	6	2	1	5	3	0	7	5	2	2	1	0	1	0	0

	Kasparov			Short			Anand			Adams			Kramnik		
	+	=	–	+	=	–	+	=	–	+	=	–	+	=	–
Karpov	20	117	26	6	13	5	4	10	5	1	2	0	1	2	0

	Kamsky			Gelfand			Ivanchuk			Shirov			Polgar		
	+	=	–	+	=	–	+	=	–	+	=	–	+	=	–
Karpov	5	3	1	3	2	1	2	9	3	2	3	0	6	2	1

	Kasparov			Karpov			Anand			Adams			Kramnik		
	+	=	–	+	=	–	+	=	–	+	=	–	+	=	–
Short	4	17	21	5	13	6	4	5	1	2	3	2	1	0	1

	Kamsky			Gelfand			Ivanchuk			Shirov			Polgar		
	+	=	–	+	=	–	+	=	–	+	=	–	+	=	–
Short	3	1	0	6	2	4	0	5	6	0	0	0	0	0	1

	Kasparov			Karpov			Short			Adams			Kramnik		
	+	=	–	+	=	–	+	=	–	+	=	–	+	=	–
Anand	3	2	5	5	10	4	1	5	4	7	7	1	0	9	0

	Kamsky			Gelfand			Ivanchuk			Shirov			Polgar		
	+	=	–	+	=	–	+	=	–	+	=	–	+	=	–
Anand	5	2	1	1	4	5	7	15	3	1	7	0	4	1	1

	Kasparov			Karpov			Short			Anand			Kramnik		
	+	=	–	+	=	–	+	=	–	+	=	–	+	=	–
Adams	0	0	1	0	2	1	2	3	2	1	7	7	1	2	0

	Kamsky			Gelfand			Ivanchuk			Shirov			Polgar		
	+	=	–	+	=	–	+	=	–	+	=	–	+	=	–
Adams	1	3	0	2	11	5	1	2	3	0	6	6	1	2	2

	Kasparov			Karpov			Short			Anand			Adams		
	+	=	–	+	=	–	+	=	–	+	=	–	+	=	–
Kramnik	2	3	1	0	2	1	1	0	1	0	9	0	0	2	1

	Kamsky			Gelfand			Ivanchuk			Shirov			Polgar		
	+	=	–	+	=	–	+	=	–	+	=	–	+	=	–
Kramnik	1	3	1	1	2	0	1	2	0	1	1	3	2	0	0

	Kasparov			Karpov			Short			Anand			Adams		
	+	=	–	+	=	–	+	=	–	+	=	–	+	=	–
Kamsky	1	2	6	1	3	5	0	1	3	1	2	5	0	3	1

	Kramnik			Gelfand			Ivanchuk			Shirov			Polgar		
	+	=	–	+	=	–	+	=	–	+	=	–	+	=	–
Kamsky	1	3	1	2	8	2	4	3	4	2	1	4	3	1	1

	Kasparov			Karpov			Short			Anand			Adams		
	+	=	–	+	=	–	+	=	–	+	=	–	+	=	–
Gelfand	0	3	5	1	2	3	4	2	6	5	4	1	5	11	2

	Kramnik			Kamsky			Ivanchuk			Shirov			Polgar		
	+	=	–	+	=	–	+	=	–	+	=	–	+	=	–
Gelfand	0	2	1	2	8	2	1	5	3	2	5	5	1	4	0

	Kasparov			Karpov			Short			Anand			Adams		
	+	=	−	+	=	−	+	=	−	+	=	−	+	=	−
Ivanchuk	2	5	7	3	9	2	6	5	0	3	15	7	3	2	1

	Kramnik			Kamsky			Gelfand			Shirov			Polgar		
	+	=	−	+	=	−	+	=	−	+	=	−	+	=	−
Ivanchuk	0	2	1	4	3	4	3	5	1	2	6	1	1	3	0

	Kasparov			Karpov			Short			Anand			Adams		
	+	=	−	+	=	−	+	=	−	+	=	−	+	=	−
Shirov	0	1	2	0	3	2	0	0	0	0	7	1	6	6	0

	Kramnik			Kamsky			Gelfand			Ivanchuk			Polgar		
	+	=	−	+	=	−	+	=	−	+	=	−	+	=	−
Shirov	3	1	1	4	1	2	5	5	2	1	6	2	1	1	0

	Kasparov			Karpov			Short			Anand			Adams		
	+	=	−	+	=	−	+	=	−	+	=	−	+	=	−
Polgar	0	0	1	1	2	6	1	0	0	1	1	4	2	2	1

	Kramnik			Kamsky			Gelfand			Ivanchuk			Shirov		
	+	=	−	+	=	−	+	=	−	+	=	−	+	=	−
Polgar	0	0	2	1	1	3	0	4	1	0	3	1	0	1	1

If these are reorganised into percentage order the results come out as follows:

Kasparov	58.36%	Kamsky	38.51%
Karpov	51.57%	Gelfand	46.32%
Short	42.48%	Ivanchuk	51.42%
Anand	54.17%	Shirov	56.35%
Adams	37.84%	Polgar	32.5%
Kramnik	51.22%		

All results to the end of May 1994 included.